Patient Care Redesign

Lessons From the Field

AONE Management Series

....

American Organization of Nurse Executives

Health Forum, Inc.
An American Hospital Association Company
CHICAGO

© 1999 by Health Forum, Inc., an American Hospital Association company. All rights reserved. No part of this publication may be reproduced, stored in a retrieval system, or transmitted, in any form or by any means, electronic, mechanical, photocopying, recording or otherwise, without the prior written permission of the publisher.

Printed in the United States of America—3/99

Cover design by Maricel Quianzon

Library of Congress Cataloging-in-Publication Data

Patient care redesign : lessons from the field / American Organization
   of Nurse Executives : Diana Weaver, editor.
      p.   cm. — (AONE management series)
   Includes index.
   ISBN 1-55648-248-5 (pkb.)
   1. Nursing services—Administration.   2. Reengineering
(Management)   I. Weaver, Diana Jane.   II. American Organization of
Nurse Executives.   III. Series.
   [DNLM: 1. Patient Care Management—organization & administration.
2. Patient Care Management—trends.   W 84.7 P2975 1999)
RT89.P3   1999
362.1'73'068—dc21
DNLM/DLC
for Library of Congress   98-53882
                                                                      CIP

Item number: 067108

Contents

About the Authors   *v*
Foreword   *ix*
Preface   *xi*

PART ONE
Introduction

CHAPTER ONE
The Patient Care Executive Role in Patient Care Redesign   *3*
Diana J. Weaver, RN, DNS, FAAN

PART TWO
Case Studies

CHAPTER TWO
*Making the Transition from Specialized Care Delivery
to a Primary Care Model*   *19*
Sue Hudec, RN, MSN, and Margaret Williams, RN, PhD

CHAPTER THREE
Restructuring to Provide Synergistic Patient Care   *49*
Peggy A. Haggerty, RN, MSN, and Mary Lu Gerke, RN, MSN

CHAPTER FOUR
Adopting the Integrated Team Management Model 71
Bonnie Michaels, RN, MA, and Mary K. Stull, RN, PhD

CHAPTER FIVE
Reengineering the Patient Care Delivery System
through Care Management 89
Norma J. Ferdinand, DNSc, MSN, RN

CHAPTER SIX
Creating High Performance through Quality Improvement 117
Mary Nolan, RN, MS

PART THREE
Lessons for the Future

CHAPTER SEVEN
Lessons Learned from the Case Study Redesign Initiatives 155
Mary E. Mancini, RN, MSN, CNA, FAAN

CHAPTER EIGHT
Impact of Today's Redesign Initiatives on Tomorrow's
Delivery of Health Care 179
Marjorie Beyers, PhD, RN, FAAN

Index 189

About the Authors

EDITOR

Diana J. Weaver, RN, DNS, FAAN, is senior clinical consultant for CSC Healthcare, Inc. Formerly, she was senior vice president for patient services at Yale-New Haven Hospital and the University of Kentucky Medical Center. She is a fellow of the American Academy of Nursing and a past president of AONE. She contributed to the book *Redesigning Healthcare Delivery* with R. Nierenberg, edited by P. Boland, in 1996. She received her MSN from Northwestern State University and DNS from Indiana University. Dr. Weaver is the recipient of distinguished alumnus awards from Indiana University School of Nursing (1995) and Ball State University (1997).

AUTHORS

Marjorie Beyers, PhD, RN, FAAN, is the executive director of the American Organization of Nurse Executives in Chicago. Previously, she was vice president, nursing and allied health systems, at Mercy Health Services, Farmington Hills, Michigan, where she provided leadership for systemwide nursing and allied health services. She has published extensively and consulted in the areas of nursing administration and quality issues in health care. In addition, she has presented more than 200 lectures to hospitals, nursing schools, and professional organizations nationwide. Dr. Beyers was the first recipient of the Roy Woodham Visiting Fellowship Award for research in the areas of financing, organization, and delivery of health services in multi-institutional systems.

Norma J. Ferdinand, DNSc (Cand.), MSN, RN, is director of care management at Lancaster General Hospital, Lancaster, Pennsylvania. She has responsibility for case management, community-based case management, social work, quality improvement, utilization management, and cardiothoracic surgery. She has extensive nursing experience in the specialty of cardiothoracic surgery. Ms. Ferdinand received her master's degree as a clinical nurse specialist in cardiopulmonary nursing from the University of Pennsylvania. She is currently working on her doctoral degree in nursing science at Widener University, Pennsylvania.

Mary Lu Gerke, RN, MSN, has been director of ICU at Gundersen Lutheran in LaCrosse, Wisconsin, for 18 years and is also director of infusion therapy and radiology. She has acted as consultant for Hewlett Packard Clinical Information System implementation and is a national and international speaker on critical care technology. She serves on several nursing boards at the local and state levels.

Peggy A. Haggerty, RN, MSN, has been director of the orthopedics/gynecology unit at Gundersen Lutheran Hospital in La Crosse, Wisconsin, for the past 11 years. She was actively involved in the implementation of the differentiated nursing roles and in the development and pilot program of the patient service assistant roles. She is a national speaker for the Bereavement/RTS Program at Gundersen Lutheran and is currently on a state nursing organization board.

Sue Hudec, RN, MSN, is associate director for patient services at the Veterans Affairs Medical Center in Washington, DC. She began her VA career as a staff nurse and has held various administrative positions at VA medical centers across the country. She has served on many VA national advisory task forces and committees and speaks at national meetings on nursing management and leadership. Ms. Hudec is a contributor to the book *Nursing Administration, Managing Patient Care* published by Appleton and Lange. She is a past board member of the American Organization of Nurse Executives. She received her MSN from the University of California at San Francisco.

Mary E. Mancini, RN, MSN, CNA, FAAN, is senior vice president of nursing administration at Parkland Health & Hospital System in Dallas, Texas. She began her career as a registered nurse at Roger Williams General Hospital in Providence, Rhode Island. Her career path has provided her with experience in a variety of health care provider settings, from staff nurse to progressive management positions in general medical/surgical nursing adult critical care and emergency services. In 1987, Ms. Mancini completed a Johnson & Johnson Wharton Nurse Executive Fellowship at the Wharton School of Business of the University of Pennsylvania. She has more than 30 publications to her credit, including three books on emergency and trauma management. She is a member of numerous nursing organizations and is a sought-after speaker both nationally and internationally.

Bonnie Michaels, RN, MA, is vice president of patient care services at Elmhurst Memorial Hospital, Elmhurst, Illinois, and a Wharton nurse executive fellow. Previously she was vice president of patient care services, All Saints Health Care, Racine, Wisconsin. Ms. Michaels has experience in hospital mergers and health care redesign and managed nursing services in academic teaching institutions and community hospital settings. She has had faculty appointments at Northwestern University and City University of New York, Hunter College.

Mary Nolan, RN, MS, is currently senior vice president of patient care and, as of March 1999, will be the general director of Albany Medical Center, Albany, New York, a top 100 hospital in 1994, 1997, and 1998. She has also held positions as director of surgical services, neuroscience nurse manager, inservice director, instructor in a school of nursing, and clinical staff nurse at Albany and other institutions. At Albany, she led the implementation of the quality improvement system, patient-centered redesign, nursing and interdisciplinary shared governance, and a number of staffing, productivity, and fiscal management systems. She has also been involved in program development and facility development. She received her MS from Russell Sage College and BSN from Molloy College.

Mary K. Stull, RN, PhD, is director of administrative and surgical services for Elmhurst Memorial Hospital in Elmhurst, Illinois. She has extensive experience in project management and worked for Northwestern Memorial Hospital, the Midwest Alliance in Nursing, the American Hospital Association, and as a health care consultant for Watson Wyatt Worldwide.

Margaret Williams, RN, PhD, is associate chief for staff development for the Washington, DC, Veterans Affairs Medical Center and is responsible for education, staffing development for patient services, and resource management. Formerly, she taught intensive care nursing and medical surgical nursing in bachelor of nursing, associate in arts, and diploma programs. She has also participated in VA national and VISN task forces. She received her certificate in nursing from Alfred University in New York and her PhD in health education from the University of Maryland.

Foreword

Nothing is more certain than the fact that the future is uncertain. Health professionals have become futurists in predicting that the rate of change will continue to increase. Change has become the currency of management competencies. Understanding change, how to manage change, and how to focus the energies of an organization on targets for performance to achieve the mission are critical competencies for executives at every level.

This book, the first of our new AONE Management Series, provides a framework for the future. The insights on what has stimulated the need to change and on how innovators around the country have responded to change are invaluable. In the future, we will be less concerned with events and more concerned with process. But the process will not concentrate on process, but on getting things done. Nurse executives are accustomed to nursing processes—and management processes. Their horizons have expanded in broadened roles and greater accountabilities for patient care.

As you read this publication, consider yourself a pioneer for the future. The learning to be gleaned is how to make transitions from one place to another; how to chart a course of action; how to build the relationships and employ the management strategies and tools that help all of the players make those transitions. Health care professionals are charting new territory in which technology and patients' participation in their own care are turning past practices upside down.

Opportunities abound to participate in building a new culture in health care. Some things will never change. Resources will always be scarce, and health care will have to compete for dollars. Some things should never change. The caring and compassion nurses provide, high standards for quality, and the concern and respect for the people who give and receive care will always be central to health care. Getting a handle on change early is a key to learning how to keep the values in the forefront, while making dramatic and significant changes in the way the work gets done. The content of this publication—the insights and lessons learned—are tools you can use in this process.

Marjorie Beyers, PhD, RN, FAAN
Executive Director
American Organization of Nurse Executives

Preface

The impetus for this book came about six years ago when I found myself in the midst of a significant redesign initiative without the aid of yardsticks or compass to guide the effort. The organization in which I was newly employed was trying to lower its operating budget by 15 percent in response to managed care penetration in the region. Past budgetary reductions had always exempted direct-care workers, and, as a result, the infrastructure of the organization had been eroded to the point that direct-care workers, particularly RNs, were performing nonclinical functions. During my initial rounds on the patient care units, staff told me they needed more help and urged me to hire more nurses to lighten their load. When I asked them about the activities that made up the majority of their workday, I learned that nurses were emptying trash, running for supplies, and performing routine transports to a variety of settings in the institution. This was my first clue that systems tinkering minus systems thinking (in this case achieving budget reductions by cutting housekeeping and supply delivery personnel), albeit well intended, resulted in more highly paid staff—RNs—picking up the work. Ironically, patient care was negatively affected, which was the very outcome that senior leadership was trying to avoid.

Although, at that time, I was not well versed in the principles of work redesign, I knew the work of patient care well enough to have a hunch about the relationships at work here. Later, as I became more fluent in redesign vocabulary, I was able to cite the principle that work will always find the path of least resistance. If it is not essential, it will simply not get done. If it is necessary, it will shift to the worker of last resort. The one who inherits the new work with little or no forewarning is sure to be resentful. The traditional solution of throwing more nurses or dollars at flawed work processes seemed a bad idea given the uphill budget battles that we were facing. Consequently, I persuaded my associates to undertake a redesign initiative. However, I was careful to emphasize that we should not exempt the patient care units. In fact, I wanted nursing and patient care to play a major role in the effort.

Why would I be advocating for a redesign project when many of my colleagues were railing against similar undertakings in their respective institutions? First, I am a pragmatist. I did not see how we could meet the financial challenges we were facing without taking this route. The hill we had to climb was too steep. Second, I had been in the field long enough to recognize that there were significant opportunities to work smarter. I have always wanted to control my own destiny. It is better to be in the driver's seat than the back seat when transformation of this magnitude is undertaken. The changing reimbursement picture provided the organizational readiness to take on this difficult but necessary rethinking of the way work was done.

However, there were no prototypes. I was consistently and appropriately challenged by nurses who pushed me for hard and fast rules and guaranteed outcomes if changes were made: What is the right skill mix of licensed to unlicensed personnel? How many hours of care are needed in the coronary care unit? When I admitted I did not know, I was met with grim looks that suggested I had sold nursing down the river. Moreover, the gravity of potential patient care consequences made this trip into the unknown very scary. But I had one thing going for me. I had worked in several different regions of the country and had networked extensively with colleagues who, because of the labor markets in their settings, could not hire all-RN staffs. They had to make do with 50, 60, or 70 percent skill mixes and still provide appropriate patient care. In other words, I knew that factors in the environment, rather than the work itself, often dictated the norm for work standards.

I soon realized that there was little in the way of systematic documentation to assist me in this journey. Business literature was helpful but generalization to patient care was not an exact fit. I needed my staff—the very people who opposed this effort—to give me clues to the right answers. My work was cut out for me, and I was not alone in this plight. Across the nation, patient care executives were trying to lead reluctant staffs to a new future without the aid of tools, knowledge of new processes and models, or benchmarking data to guide their efforts.

This book describes the creation and implementation of patient care redesigns that reduced costs, improved patient care, and enhanced the worklife of hospital staffs. Part 1, "Introduction," consists of one chapter that describes the evolution of redesign from the early slash-and-burn labor reduction approaches to the prevailing and, I hope, somewhat more enlightened philosophy of today, which focuses on simplifying and streamlining clinical work. The goal is to achieve a balance of the right work or intervention at the right place and time provided by the right caregiver at the right cost, to produce the desired patient outcomes. Chapter 1 also discusses the necessary melding of clinical and operational imperatives so that finance is not the dog wagging the patient care tail.

Part 2, "Case Studies," consists of five chapters focusing on different health care organizations that have successfully implemented a work redesign. In bringing about change, all these organizations had one overarching similarity—they all had a vision. Every change begins with an idea, a notion that the future can and must be created. It is the soul of leadership. As you read the case studies, you will note the role that vision plays as leaders act and react in their particular circumstances.

The five case studies illustrate the long-held tenet that all health care is local, while providing global themes regarding the necessary ingredients for successful redesign. They also highlight the inevitable bumps in the road that come with complex change efforts involving hundreds of people and processes. The authors have written their stories with a candor and openness that allow the reader to share vicariously in the redesign experience. This level of honesty is essential for true learning to take place, but it is counter to the past culture, which was often referred to as the "liar's club" because no one wanted to admit to a colleague that failures abound in an environment where all the rules are suspended—permanently!

In part 3, "Lessons for the Future," chapter 7 discusses the themes or principles that thread throughout the preceding case studies. These principles provide the bedrock for any redesign initiative; but in a broader context, these themes could be argued to be the fabric of strategic leadership in today's health care environment. Indeed, they provide a framework for leading and sustaining major changes.

Chapter 8 is predictive in nature. If the themes illustrated by the case studies and described in chapter 7 hold true, what are their implications for clinical and managerial education? What knowledge will we need to shorten process improvement cycles, become more skillful and efficient in our clinical and operational processes, and still further the science of evidence-based care management? Will policy begin to capture the necessary holistic nature of health care instead of reacting to special interests that voice legitimate specific concerns but often disturb the balance of our health care ecosystem?

For those of us who have dedicated our lives to caring for others, the answers to the questions above must be pursued. We may not know the answers, but we know the potential penalties for not asking the questions. And that is sufficient motivation for most of us!

Diana J. Weaver, RN, DNS, FAAN

PART ONE

Introduction

CHAPTER ONE

The Patient Care
Executive Role
in Patient Care Redesign

Diana J. Weaver, RN, DNS, FAAN

There have been more ups and downs in health care during
the 1990s, especially in the hospital environment, than in a day
on the roller coaster at Coney Island. Hospitals, the most
prominent players in the health care delivery system, have been
scrambling to remain viable in the face of increased financial
pressures brought on by managed care. One strategy that was
viewed with both great expectations and great consternation,
depending on one's place in the organizational hierarchy, was
the introduction of the systematic change labeled "work
redesign." The concept of work redesign is based on the principles of total quality management, multidisciplinary teams,
and work simplification. Its early application was met with
great resistance from nursing staff, who viewed the terms
redesign and *job loss* as interchangeable. However, redesign now
is viewed as a work in progress in virtually every hospital
across the nation. What forces created the need for patient care
redesign? What role does the individual who is ultimately
responsible for patient care, the nursing executive, play in the
redesign process? And, finally, what are the necessary dynamics

3

in successful, sustained organizational change that make the preferred future a reality?

This chapter describes the major social, societal, medical, economic, and cultural factors that spawned the fee-for-service model of health care that prevailed in the United States before managed care. It discusses the focus of early applications of work redesign and the resulting backlash by nursing. It goes on to explain the role of the patient care executive in executing redesign that integrates clinical, operational, and financial elements of patient care and accomplishes the strategic intent of true redesign.

Factors Contributing to the Fee-for-Service Reimbursement Environment

According to De Pree, the role of the leader is to define reality.[1] But what is the reality of health care these days? It isn't what it used to be, and the emerging reality has created a significant dilemma for those caregivers who are products of the very comfortable, albeit costly, fee-for-service (FFS) reimbursement environment. In that environment, they provided services—predominantly in acute care settings—that were believed to be inherently good.

The factors that contributed to this model for care delivery in the United States were societal, cultural, medical, and economic in scope. America was founded on a belief in rugged individualism, hence the rights of the individual were of greater value than the rights of the collective. Consequently, clinicians were socialized to their respective professions under the philosophy that all efforts should be made to prolong life and save the person, with little or no regard for the cost or ultimate quality-of-life outcomes. Health care providers in this country have long believed in and practiced the tenet that the quality of medical care was a function of the number and caliber of interventions or resources used.[2] No one really worried about the escalating financial implications of illness care that was delivered in hospitals across the nation. Dramatic interventions that saved the day and/or the individual are hallmarks of our culture. Life itself was the goal.

From the public health perspective, health care providers have been able to lengthen life expectancy by improving sanitation and conquering infectious diseases that robbed Americans of their children well into the twentieth century. However, as health care economists have noted (and systems thinking affirms), medical breakthroughs of the past created the clinical challenges of the present. Increased longevity now means that the chronic conditions of an aging society must be dealt with. Quick surgical fixes and magic antibiotics no longer work for a large majority of Americans. Instead, care needs to be palliative and supportive. This mode of care does not fit with the acute care model, nor is it well understood or embraced by clinicians who have been schooled in episodic care.

Finally, capitalism undergirds all aspects of the American economy, including health care delivery. Spending money on acute care was considered the right approach to managing the health of the populace. And until the very recent past, the protective layer of indemnity insurance effectively insulated most people from the realities of the cost of care. It was almost like playing with monopoly money from the vantage point of patient and provider. However, critical global factors are forcing us to revisit all of our assumptions, including those that have shaped our health care system.

Introduction of the Work Redesign Effort

During the past decade, technology and information systems have made international trade commonplace. With the initiation of a global economy, it is just as easy for the U.S. consumer to buy a Honda as a Ford—and often the Honda is cheaper. To compete effectively in a global marketplace, big business in the United States began scrutinizing the variables that made up its cost structure. Health care premiums, which had gone unchecked for years, were at the top of the list. It did not take long for executive leadership to understand that the FFS model was no longer affordable. In addition, they began to demand that accountability be built into health care practices. These were the new rules of the game. Being held accountable for the clinical outcomes and the cost of services constituted a sea change for health care in this country. After big business realized that it could exert clout and exact savings by negotiating lower rates, the rules of the game were completely and permanently changed.

Facing this reality, hospital administrators and their boards began to look for quick ways to reduce the costs of patient care delivery. They noted that their counterparts in business and industry were engaged in a process called work redesign in an effort to reduce payrolls and increase productivity. The Japanese were the earliest champions of this approach, and the results were impressive. Work redesign was based on a set of principles incorporating the philosophy of total quality improvement, which was engaged in by cross-functional work teams empowered to simplify processes and eliminate work. Health care administrators were eager to talk with health care consultants, who promised significant labor savings with their new product—patient-focused care.

Hospitals are labor-intensive environments, and the highest percentage of the labor dollars are in nursing cost-centers. Thus, it was not surprising that nursing care was the first system targeted for redesign. Moreover, because nursing care delivery is a process and not an outcome, the practice has been not only poorly understood by those outside the profession, but also inadequately defined and quantified by those within it. The result has been an undervaluing of the work of nursing—even by nurses—and a lack of appreciation for the complexity of patient care. To make matters even more difficult, early redesign initiatives were sometimes implemented in a "burning platform" environment, which resulted when hospitals were hemorrhaging financially. In these circumstances, registered nurses (RNs) were taken out of the workforce rapidly and in large numbers, and unlicensed personnel were inserted into the caregiver complement.

The response to this approach from organized nursing was swift and, in the main, negative. Concerns were raised about patient safety and RN job security. Managed care and patient care redesign were both labeled "the enemy" by nursing staffs across the country. Their anxiety about both was quickly shared by the physician community and, ultimately, the public at large. Some of the negative publicity about early redesign efforts may have been warranted because clinical issues were often glossed over in deference to achieving financial goals. But, to be fair, survival was the overriding priority for many of these hospitals.

Attributes of the Patient Care Executive Role in Successful Work Redesign

As with all change, the process of redesign is neither all good nor all bad. The deciding factors are in the execution, not the principles! The patient care executive (PCE) must serve as the linchpin for successful patient care design initiatives. This statement will not surprise nurses or physicians (usually), but may not be as self-evident to other members of an organization's senior leadership team. The reasons that the PCE can make or break this important endeavor are directly related to the continuous nature of patient care in the acute care setting.

To date, the only clinician who is consistently present in the patient care environment is the nurse. With patient care increasing in complexity, new clinical roles have emerged— respiratory therapists, child life specialists, social workers, to name but a few. These are all roles that were notably absent in the acute care setting before 1950. At that time, the patient care unit was a nursing care unit, period. As caregivers in the new roles became important members of the care delivery team, it became easy to overlook the fact that nursing serves as the base for all care delivered in the acute care setting. The nurse is the integrator of the plan of care and, consequently, nursing provides the contextual environment in which all other clinicians operate. Little wonder, then, that the nurse executive must serve as the linchpin for patient care redesign because his or her vantage point is the only one that captures the entire fabric of care delivery.

For a work redesign to be successful, the PCE must take on certain responsibilities. He or she must do the following:

- Challenge assumptions about the work
- Create an adaptive environment
- Encourage systems thinking
- Coach the first-line managers

Challenging Assumptions about the Work

The level of commitment and involvement of the clinical leadership, particularly the PCE, has a great impact on the success of the work redesign. When PCEs are notably absent or do not take an active role in championing the new vision and working in partnership with patient care staff and physicians, redesign can became a pseudonym for budget cuts. On the other hand, when nursing leaders push everyone, including themselves, to critically assess the work of patient care as it is currently done, many flawed or unnecessary aspects of work are identified. Frequently, staff offer excellent solutions for problems they have noted for some time as they have gone about their daily work routines. However, they have not pursued their ideas for improvement because, as they frankly admit, no one has ever told them they could or should! Often the environment is replete with inefficiencies that have sprouted from real or perceived needs of first-line workers as they struggle with unresponsive or broken systems.

One example of such inefficiency is when RNs take time to clean beds to expedite patient admissions. The fact is that bedside nurses, who have been professionally socialized to do everything necessary to ensure good patient care, may not recognize this as an inefficient practice that only perpetuates the problem. Such an activity not only diverts the RN's energy and time away from patient care, it is also a wasteful use of the hospital's labor dollars. If staff nurses do not critically evaluate their expertise as a scarce resource to be conserved for patient care (which no one else can provide), they will continue to do everything they perceive to be needed to render patient care. In the work redesign concept, systems thinking informs us that it is imperative to involve all workers who participate in the processes that make up patient care. All assumptions, rituals, and practices must be scrutinized and tough questions asked about their efficacy.

Creating an Adaptive Environment

One of the PCE's important but often overlooked responsibilities is to educate staff and colleagues on the importance of turning the patient care environment into a self-organizing system that can be highly adaptive in this time of unprecedented change. Wheatley assigns three attributes to organizational adaptation: self-awareness, plentiful sensing devices, and a strong capacity for reflection.[3] These attributes, which are in dynamic equilibrium with each other, can serve as helpful indicators of patient care services' readiness for change and redesign work. One approach is for the PCE to involve the patient care leadership team in answering certain questions regarding each of the three adaptation attributes:

- *Self-awareness:* This attribute allows for self-definition of role and core competencies.
  —Do RNs and other clinicians have a clear sense of professional/role identity?
  —Do job descriptions contain role definition and delineation statements with competencies identified?

—Are staff aware of the impact of their individual expertise on patient care?

—Can staff describe the interrelationships of multiple roles in task completion?

- *Plentiful sensing devices:* This attribute provides multiple information sources that influence the organizational environment.

  —Are staff given periodic updates of factors in the external environment that affect the institution?

  —Are the organization's long-term strategic plan and the annual business plan/goals shared with all staff, with discussion of the impact of each on the individual work units?

  —Are key fiscal and operational metrics reported regularly and shared with staff?

  —Do clinical quality improvement initiatives use external benchmarking data for internal reference and goal setting?

  —Are key financial, operational, and clinical indicators tracked for variance, and are the data shared with staff?

  —Are individual and team performance reviews based on predetermined outcomes?

- *Strong capacity for reflection:* This attribute ensures self-examination of values, assumptions, and current practices.

  —Have staff been offered opportunities to question changes in practice and processes?

  —Is some form of shared governance in place so that staff serve on committees and other decision-making bodies?

  —Are all staff expected to develop annual goals and complete self-evaluations?

Environmental adaptation requires that a history of mutual trust, dialogue, and respect exists between the PCE and the patient care staff. Staff members need to be encouraged to ask questions about their work and its impact on the total organization, with the goal of helping them grasp the interrelationships in care delivery. If caregivers understand how patient care is paid for, they are much more likely to be good stewards of the resources within their control. Further, they will be prepared to objectively evaluate the fiscal message at the time of redesign. Moreover, staff who have had ample opportunity to explore new ways to do their work are likely to be an invaluable source of ideas for improving work processes.

Encouraging Systems Thinking

Successful redesign initiatives require an understanding of and appreciation for systems thinking. Simply stated, systems thinking identifies internal and external elements and influences within the work environment and seeks to understand their interrelatedness. The nursing unit and the financial office are inseparable parts of the same whole. Without a grasp of this phenomenon, redesign may cause irreparable damage to the fragile patient care delivery system. And it is the PCE's responsibility to educate senior leadership, direct caregivers, and support staff to that reality.

A related responsibility resting on the PCE's shoulders is that of communicating and interpreting the perspectives of each member of the senior leadership team to the patient care staff. All the members of the senior leadership team play a unique and important role in crafting the strategic plan for the organization and implementing the aspects of the plan that are within their responsibility and control. Thus, knowledge of each of the roles within the senior leadership team is important to the rank and file staff who often hold stereotypic and sometimes negative views of the different positions, especially when redesign is being launched. For example, the CEO is ultimately accountable for operationalizing the vision of the organization. The chief financial officer must ensure that those resources needed—and no more—are the ones used to make the organization's vision a reality. The human resources officer serves as caretaker of the most vital resource any health care facility possesses—its people.

Helping staff gain an appreciation of the various administrative roles and their interplay in the organizational dynamics will give them a sense of predictability at a time when their world seems to be out of control. And they are not as likely to label individuals as the "bad guys" if they are, in fact, being true to their organizational roles.

Coaching the First-Line Managers

The work of patient care has undergone little systematic scrutiny in the past. With the advent of redesign, we as nurses have begun to examine our own practices in health care, from both the operational and clinical perspectives. To some in the field, this is a very scary proposition, and they often react by canonizing the past. All of a sudden, yesterday's way of doing things was perfect. The very act of questioning seems to suggest that one is disloyal to health care or nursing values. It is imperative that the patient care executive coach others, particularly the nurse managers at the unit level, through this logic barrier. If this cannot be achieved, the entire process of redesign, which is essentially cerebral, will be flawed and likely fail.

The interaction between the leader and those who bear the front-line responsibility for care delivery is a dance of sorts. The lead in the dance must change hands as the information flows back and forth. The nurse manager and the direct-care staff know the nature of the work as it currently exists. They also understand the care needs of the patient population they serve. However, they have seldom had to define these needs in a logical, sequential manner. Nor have they examined relationships between and among their roles, care activities, and patient needs. It is the PCE's responsibility to help managers organize the knowledge they possess and to formulate hypotheses for the improvement of care delivery to maximize quality and cost goals.

Essence of True Redesign

Initially, patient care redesign was focused on the operational aspects of care delivery. Like the five rights of medication administration, redesign espoused the rights in care delivery: the right care, at the right place, by the right provider, at the right time, with the right outcome, at the right cost. Several elements of this equation suggest a clinical quality imperative; however, the bulk of the redesign effort was centered on downward substitution of work and/or revamping the work itself. Case management and critical pathways were usually discussed, but were often given short shrift in the total project. The reason for this was fairly straightforward. Critical pathway development and implementation were dependent on physician buy-in to the process, and physicians, unlike hospital employees, did not initially have to comply with the goals of redesign. However, as managed care began to capture more and more covered lives, physicians began to see their professional care case-managed by external case managers who served as agents for the HMOs. Many clinicians foresaw this intrusion on clinical practice by the payers and, seeking to control their own destinies, began the process of case management in cooperation with the hospital. The question became one of "Shall I define case management on my terms or will someone else define it for me," and enlightened physicians chose the former.

Today, a core of practicing physicians, in partnership with patient care leaders, have begun to ask the key questions about clinical interventions and their effectiveness in managing disease and/or promoting health. Some questions are broad and far-reaching in terms of current practice. For example, "Which clinical interventions account for the key desired patient outcomes?"

Or, "Why do physician-ordering practices for similar medical diagnoses vary by region of the country?" Other questions are much more focused on care specifics; for example, "What is the relationship between early ambulation and acute care length of stay in patients with joint replacement?" Low-cost alternatives to care, from generic drugs to lifestyle changes such as moderate exercise, are beginning to be accepted by patients, endorsed by physicians, and championed by payers. In addition, we are now beginning to understand not only what a particular intervention should be, but also how much it should cost and when it should be implemented for utmost efficacy.

Conclusion

When hospital administrations first began to adapt the work redesign concept from business and industry, front-line staff, particularly caregivers, saw the effort as a step toward devaluing the role of nursing and undercutting the quality of health care delivery. However, in time, the concept began to be accepted as integral to the emerging delivery models and not just an effort to improve the bottom line. Today, everyone within the health care organization has a role to play in the process of work redesign, but no one is more key to its success than the patient care executive. It is this position that pulls together the various functions involved in care delivery and helps each one to understand and appreciate the other's participation. To succeed, she or he must assume a number of new responsibilities, including that of educating staff and administrators on the importance of creating a self-organizing system and encouraging staff to think in terms of systems.

As clinical guidelines with associated care processes are refined and their use becomes accepted practice, true redesign will begin to take shape. Meanwhile, as we all struggle mightily to survive and prosper, do we hear a murmuring Darwin saying something about those organisms better adapted to the environment surviving—and those least fitted, not?

References

1. M. De Pree, *Leadership Is an Art* (Garden City, NY: Doubleday, 1989), p. 9.

2. I. Morrison, *The Second Curve* (New York: Ballantine Books, 1996), p. 184.

3. M. J. Wheatley, *Leadership and the New Science* (San Francisco: Berrett-Koehler, 1992).

PART TWO

Case Studies

CHAPTER TWO

Making the Transition from Specialized Care Delivery to a Primary Care Model

Sue Hudec, RN, MSN
Margaret Williams, RN, PhD

In 1994, the Veterans Affairs Medical Center (VAMC) in Washington, DC, had 579 acute care beds and 120 nursing home beds.[1] There were approximately 214,000 clinic visits (once in 24 hours), with 341,000 individual encounters (involving various disciplines and/or providers).[2] Off-site, there was a methadone maintenance clinic and two veterans centers (psychological counseling "storefront" centers). In addition to the clinical program, there were active education and research programs. It was and is the only medical center in the VA system to maintain affiliations with three schools of medicine. The VAMC also had educational agreements with eight allied health professions and a research budget of approximately $9.5 million.

This case study describes the VAMC before and during the planning and implementation of a new care model. It emphasizes the transitional processes required to move a large tertiary care medical center from specialized care delivery to primary care delivery.

Organizational Culture before the Change to Primary Care

Before implementation of the current primary care model, the medical center was very much like most academic centers throughout the country. Its systems and processes were organized to meet the requirements of the medical training programs and for the convenience of the providers. Care was specialized, fragmented, uncoordinated, and mostly delivered in an inpatient setting. For any and all problems, patients were encouraged to report to the center, where they saw a cast of thousands and were often confronted with new faces at each visit. If a patient needed to be admitted, it was to the ward that was designated to accept new admissions that day, rarely to a team or a consistent provider. All unscheduled patient visits were processed through the Ambulatory Evaluation Clinic with wait times sometimes up to 12 hours.

Within the organization, some departments (generally the clinical services, including nursing) reported to the chief of staff and others (generally the administrative services) reported to an associate director. Each department (service) functioned independently. Values were not clearly addressed across the medical center, and each service interpreted and developed its own values and mission statement as appropriate. Nursing Service developed values, mission, and goals by including all staff, whereas other services developed their values and mission unilaterally. Like other medical centers at the time, the VAMC had no published values and/or mission statement. Thus, there was no consistent culture regarding patient care.

Staff believed patients would automatically return to the center because they had no alternative to the VA system, and were secure in their positions because reductions in force (RIFs) were unknown in the VA at the time. Also, VA medical centers were known for having fewer staff than the private sector. From the administrative viewpoint, federal regulations made it difficult to remove unproductive individuals from their positions. There was a collective-bargaining presence in the medical center, with three unions and three different contracts representing professional and nonprofessional employees. The unions' primary role was to counsel and represent staff in grievance procedures invoked as a result of disciplinary actions. The American Federation of Government Employees (AFGE) represented nonprofessional and nonsupervisory General Schedule employees, the Laborers International Union of North American (LIUNA) represented the Wage Grade employees, and the American Nurses Association (ANA) represented professional nurses. The unions were consulted when there were anticipated changes in work conditions, but generally not when there were to be clinical program changes.

In 1994, there was minimal monitoring of critical processes; quality assurance, rather than continuous improvement, was the methodology in use across the medical center. Little attention was paid to the costs of care, and few systems were in place to determine costs. Bed days of care, bed utilization, and the need to shift care to the outpatient setting were not yet part of the center's performance standards. Emphasis was on controlling increases in costs rather than decreasing them. A complex national system was in place to allocate the annual budget to the individual medical centers. Within the medical center, service chiefs were empowered to be fiscally responsible for funding control points under their management. Resource/fiscal decisions were generally made at the service level but were uncoordinated; duplication and waste often resulted. Locally, Nursing Service managed its human resources budget, but no other services wanted this responsibility. The Resources Committee managed the full-time-equivalent (FTE) budget for the other departments of the medical center by monitoring the number of positions within a service and controlling recruitment and employment dates.

Overall staffing for Nursing Service was approximately 66 percent registered nurses (RNs), 15 percent licensed practical nurses (LPNs), and 19 percent nursing assistants (NAs).[3] Training programs for NAs were managed by the Nursing Education Department, and there were national standards for mandated hours of training for promotion and assumption of more complex procedures. Recruitment was easy, with the exception of the ICUs. Nurses were generally assigned to a specific ward and became highly specialized. They rarely were required to cover outside their own ward. Staff were assigned to either inpatient units or to outpatient clinics and were not used interchangeably. There was an emphasis on being a member of a nursing team, but no emphasis on being a member of an interdisciplinary team. However, Nursing Service was recognized as progressive and able to get the job done. Typically, the joke around the medical center was: "If you want to get it done, get a nurse."

Impetus for Change

Historically, the health care for more than 30,000 veteran patients across the Washington, DC, area was managed by physician specialists through a series of clinics, subspecialties, and inpatient services at this VAMC. Patients were cared for by a number of physicians, depending on current diagnosis, condition, or need at a particular point in time. Although the Joint Commission on Accreditation of Healthcare Organizations and the Occupational Safety and Health Administration consistently indicated that the methods of care delivery were excellent, internal reviews indicated that the cost of care was higher than desirable and continuity of care fell short of the growing expectations in health care. Also during this time (late 1993), the VA headquarters mandated that every medical center develop an approach to managed care.[4] This directive emphasized that costs across the VA medical centers were not in line with the private sector, and future planning should consider a more cost-effective care delivery system. In addition, an audit of local patients by the Inspector General from VA headquarters revealed that some patients could not identify their personal patient care provider and were not consistently satisfied with their care.

In November 1993, the nurse executive participated in a regional educational conference that provided information and expert guidance on developing managed care, as well as examples of VAs that had already started primary care.[5-8] With this impetus, she and the chief of medicine began to explore models of care that would be appropriate for the center's patient population and to the mission, vision, and goals of the larger VA system. A review of literature showed that private-sector health care was moving toward primary care—the foundation of managed care. The question was how to bring about the change to primary care in this academically oriented medical center. In addition to causing a shift in care delivery, the change would affect the psyche of the clinical staff and patients, taking them from a high-comfort system to a more efficient, streamlined system of delivering and receiving care. Yet another problem was how to provide adequate clinical opportunities for the three affiliated medical schools.

With these challenges facing the nurse executive, she chose to rely on a broad approach found in the nursing and business literature and recommended these management projects:[9-13]

- Define the purpose of primary care in the VAMC setting and describe it as fully as possible
- Assess the past culture and the changes needed to move to primary care
- Identify processes and achievements required to make the change to primary care happen
- Address ways to help nursing function effectively in a primary care environment

The nurse executive and the chief of medicine began to resolve the issue of defining the purpose by investigating primary care models in similar settings. It soon became apparent that their VAMC had some unique characteristics in terms of setting, patient population, and services that had to be considered. The definition of primary care for this medical center had to be consistent with VA directives and reflect how primary care could best be interpreted and delivered within the local setting. With this caveat, primary care was defined as the coordinated, interdisciplinary provision of comprehensive health care, consisting of intake; initial assessment; health promotion; disease prevention; emergency services (commensurate with the facility capability); management of acute and chronic biopsychosocial conditions; referrals for specialty, rehabilitation, and other levels of care; follow-up; overall care management; and patient and caregiver education.[14] This definition drove model development and helped determine the boundaries of the primary care project.

As the primary care model developed, the nurse executive firmly held to the belief that it must deliver coordinated care more effectively and be more cost efficient than the inpatient model currently in place. In addition, she believed the model should include the following elements:

- A self-directed work-team approach
- Patient-centered care
- Hospitalwide implementation using continuous quality improvement
- Cost-effective use of available resources

The nurse executive also understood that an organization with a long history of one style of care delivery and management would need time and intense effort to adjust to a change as drastic as altering the care delivery system and its organizational management.

The objective of the change to primary care was to improve care by implementing a primary care model that identified patient groups and provided care that was competent, accessible, continuous, and comprehensive. The tertiary capacity of the VAMC was to be maintained. The model was to sustain the research and educational functions, and it was to be resource neutral. Furthermore, it was to provide each patient with a provider and a primary care team the patient would know and that would provide continuity of care across time and place.

Planning Phase

After reaching a shared vision regarding a primary care model that would incorporate both outpatient and inpatient care, the nurse executive and chief of medicine discussed the need to implement such a model with the chief of staff. In February 1994, he directed them to begin planning a model of primary care that would be dynamic, address changes in the health care delivery system, and meet the needs of veteran patients.

Establishment of the Primary Care Planning/Implementation Group

A Primary Care Planning/Implementation Group chaired by the chief of medicine and the nurse executive was established. This group designed and implemented virtually all aspects of the new care system and ensured that all changes supported high-quality care. Membership in the group included all stakeholders: the clinical bed service chiefs (medicine, surgery, neurology, and psychiatry) as well as the associate chief of staff for geriatrics and extended care, and the chiefs of medical administration, social work, and information resources management. Other individuals were chosen because of systems that would have to be changed (such as laboratory and radiology). The associate chief of Nursing Service for Research and the chiefs of Engineering and Fiscal Services became part of the group because of their needed expertise and their individually expressed interest.

The group was given the power needed to bring about the required changes and was responsible for the major decision making. Decisions requiring formal approval were submitted to the appropriate medical center committees for final approval, and the chief of staff and the medical center director were kept informed as plans developed.

Appointment of an RN Project Coordinator

Early on, the nurse executive realized that the task would require a full-time project coordinator. A supervisory nurse who was a respected leader was reassigned to work directly with the nurse executive and the chief of medicine on the project's planning and implementation. She assumed the role of RN project coordinator and became a member of the planning/implementation group. Finally, because of the anticipated major shift from inpatient to outpatient care, the assistant chief of medicine for ambulatory care also joined the group.

The group identified five areas for research and development: staff education, patient education, space, informatics, and evaluation. Five subgroups were established, each headed by a member of the original planning/implementation group. The subgroups were expected to research primary care in their respective areas, consult with the appropriate individuals, and bring issues and recommendations back to the Primary Care Planning/Implementation Group for decision making and time frames for completion.

Development of a Primary Care Implementation Plan

An implementation plan was developed that encompassed the definition of primary care, criteria for primary care groups, assignment of patients to groups, staff and patient education, start dates, evaluation criteria, and plans for ongoing monitoring and continuous improvement. The chief of medicine and the nurse executive predicted that five years would be required for a complete transition to primary care. That was deemed sufficient time to recruit formally trained primary care providers, put total information systems in place, reassign all patients from specialty clinics into primary care clinics, and so on.

The beginning date of July 1, 1995, was selected for two reasons: it was the start of a new academic year when new residents and interns began their rotations, and it provided the time required to get most systems in place. From March 1994 until July 1995, there was a flurry of activity in preparation for the transition to a new patient care delivery model. For the most part, time frames were met, but dates constantly needed to be reassessed and plans reevaluated as other changes occurred within the medical center. During this same period, Nursing Service began a process to support and complement the Primary Care Planning/Implementation Group. Nursing Service established four task forces to investigate and develop the following:

1. Roles and responsibilities
2. Team building
3. Operations
4. Required staff education

Concurrently, there was new leadership of the ANA, the AFGE, and the LIUNA local chapters, along with increased government emphasis on partnership with unions. Because of the anticipated changes in work conditions associated with primary care and the new emphasis on partnerships, dialogue between management and the unions occurred on a more regular basis, allowing the changes to proceed smoothly.

The chief of staff appointed a separate group to make recommendations on how to maintain our tertiary, education, and research missions as we moved to primary care. The nurse executive was an active member of this group, which made recommendations on ways the affiliating schools of medicine could benefit from the practice of primary care. It was clear that any systems changes would require the buy-in and support of our affiliates, because the Washington, DC, VAMC provided a major training site for interns and residents.

Resource Assessment

Resources were assessed during the planning phase. The transition was to be budget neutral; therefore, existing resources needed to be redistributed from inpatient services to outpatient services and new programs being developed to support primary care. Because there was no increase in resources, all individuals involved had to incorporate their primary care activities into their current assignments. No external consultants were used. However, as a benefit of the VA system, staff were able to seek advice and assistance from other VAs as well as from academic and professional colleagues. But even though these sources provided important information, there was very little field experience reported on developing an outpatient/inpatient model of primary care, or on a model that incorporated psychiatry and neurology primary care. Thus, it was necessary to rely on staff expertise to plan and implement these parts of the model. The formal planning lasted approximately five months; however, planning for refinements continued throughout the implementation phase and is ongoing even today.

Description of the Model

Four discrete primary care groups of approximately 5,000 patients were identified for internal medicine. In recognizing that specific patients with certain chronic illnesses would always require providers with expertise in those illnesses, psychiatry, neurology, and geriatrics/extended care each formed an additional primary care group of approximately 1,500 to 3,000 patients. The decision to include psychiatry and neurology was unique and experimental, and these services were required to provide the same level of care as was provided in the general medical clinics. It was decided these seven primary care groups would be supported through interdisciplinary self-directed work teams. Each team would include a physician and a nurse as co-leaders, a physician, nurses, nurse practitioner, physician assistant, social worker, dietitian, clinical pharmacist, and administrative staff along with allied health support. Matrix organization would be used to manage the primary care teams to improve team-work and interpersonal relationships as well as to increase communication between the inpatient and outpatient areas. Staff assigned to a primary care team would be accountable to a dual line of authority. Functionally, they would report to a service (such as social work) and, programmatically, to the primary care group co-leaders. The service chief would provide support for the scope of practice, professional standards, competencies, and role development. The primary care group co-leaders would coordinate the efforts of the specialized staff from the various services and negotiate with the service chiefs to meet the needs of the primary care patients.

Social Security numbers would be used to assign veterans to one of the four medical groups, while patients for psychiatry, geriatrics/extended care, and neurology would be identified based on diagnosis, age, and/or functionality. Once patients were assigned to a primary care group, they would receive most of their outpatient/inpatient care from members of their assigned interdisciplinary team. Each primary care team became responsible for a 30- to 35-bed inpatient unit, a daily walk-in or urgent clinic, and regularly scheduled clinics. To help patients remember their group, each team selected a color designator. When there was a disagreement about which "color" group to assign a patient, the medical record was referred to a "Rainbow Committee" for assignment to the appropriate primary care group. Figure 2-1 shows the structure of the interdisciplinary team organization within the primary care model.

Figure 2-1. Structure of Primary Care Interdisciplinary Teams

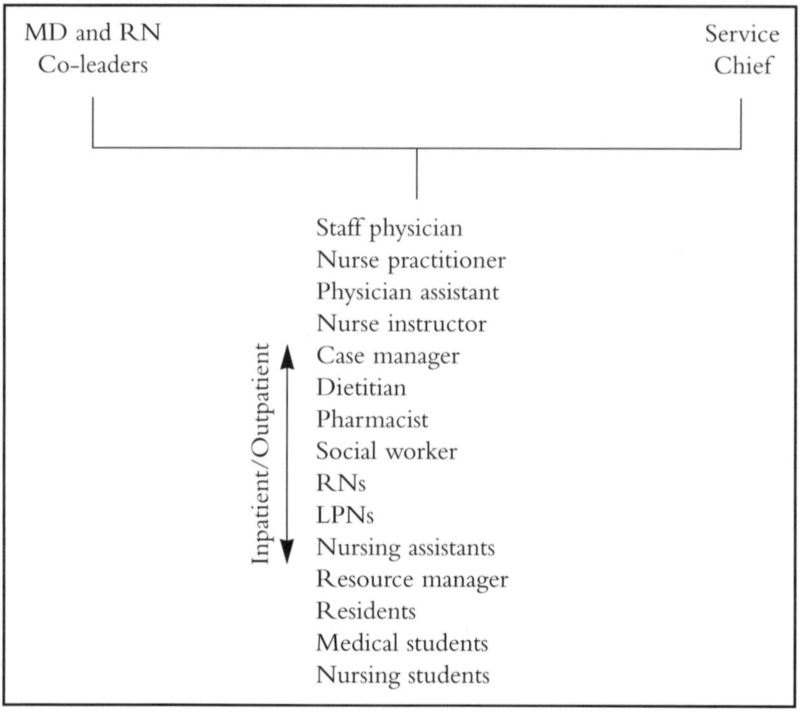

MD and RN Co-leaders	Service Chief

Inpatient/Outpatient

Staff physician
Nurse practitioner
Physician assistant
Nurse instructor
Case manager
Dietitian
Pharmacist
Social worker
RNs
LPNs
Nursing assistants
Resource manager
Residents
Medical students
Nursing students

Transition/Implementation Phase

The Primary Care Planning/Implementation Group continued to work to ensure the center's readiness for the change to primary care. Key staff at the medical center made sure that all possible tasks were accomplished, and on July 1, 1995, the center converted to a fully functioning primary care delivery system.

Implementation Tasks, Responsibilities, and Decisions

The nurse executive's unique position and administrative skills, in-depth knowledge of local and national administrative issues, and commitment to the primary care concept placed her in a key position to initiate and drive the elements necessary to bring about the change. In recognition of her vision, competence, and exceptional effectiveness, her position was elevated to associate director for patient services in October 1994. Although not an initial part of the primary care plan, this elevation became essential in fully implementing the model.

The RN project coordinator was an important player in the implementation process. She became responsible for the day-to-day activities associated with the redesign. Her familiarity with the VA system, medical center, and formal and informal power structures enabled her to negotiate the work that needed to be done. She met daily with both the nurse executive and weekly with the Primary Care Planning/Implementation Group. Her belief in the project and ability to promote and sell the transition was extremely beneficial as she communicated the importance of the project throughout the medical center.

Appointment of Co-leaders for Primary Care Teams

The following process was designed to select nursing co-leaders for the four primary care groups: a master's degree was required, skills and required experience were announced, and screened applicants were interviewed by senior nursing management, who then made recommendations to the nurse executive. After this, interviews were arranged with the chiefs of the clinical bed services responsible for each of the primary care groups. The chiefs of psychiatry, neurology, and geriatrics/extended care quickly concurred with nursing recommendations. The chief of medicine agreed with the recommendations after some discussion regarding the assignments and how to deal with current nurse managers who did not qualify for the co-leader positions. Fortunately, the co-leaders chosen proved to be very good matches. They were responsible for writing new policies to support primary care and to review and revise current policies and procedures to reflect the new care delivery system.

Work of the Subgroups

As mentioned earlier, subgroups of the Primary Care Planning/Implementation Group were formed to work on five areas needing research and development. The following subsections discuss the work of each of these subgroups.

Staff Education Subgroup   The staff education subgroup designed an educational program for the physicians and advanced practice nurses on management of primary care patients. The Nursing Education Department developed a course for direct-care workers to accomplish the following:

- To understand primary care as it was to be implemented in this medical center
- To identify and explain the new organizational structure for primary care
- To identify the changing role of health care
- To explain the advantages of primary care to patients and staff

The concept of change and how change may affect all staff were reviewed. Staff were encouraged to identify ways they could assist one another with the implementation of primary care. New roles and activities for the co-leaders, staff, case managers, and interdisciplinary team members were discussed.

Staff members needed to develop new competencies, particularly inpatient nursing staff assigned to assume responsibilities in the outpatient clinics. For example, psychiatric inpatient nurses who previously did not care for patients with IVs and medical problems now had to be trained in IV therapy and other medical nursing care procedures, since our definition of primary care included care of the whole patient.

Patient Education Subgroup   Patient education was considered critical to the model's success. Patient focus groups were conducted to obtain patient input. Like some staff members, some patients were also anxious and hesitant about the change. Many had considered the subspecialist "their" physician and were not very excited about primary care. Also, patients liked being seen by a number of specialists and the ability to self-refer to specialty clinics rather than going through a primary care provider.

To address these changes, the chief of medicine and nurse executive, as well as key physicians and nurses, met with veteran service organizations to inform them of the coming changes, elicit their comments, and educate their members (our patients) about the changes. For the past 40 years, VA patients had been told to come to the medical center for any health or social problems they encountered. Now, they were being asked to call for an appointment or call a medical advice line before coming to the center. Most of the service organizations liked the proposal, but some individuals needed to be convinced of the advantages of having a primary care provider.

The patient education subgroup wrote articles about the changes for the Veterans newsletter. Flyers were developed and placed in strategic locations throughout the medical center. Clinical staff developed attractive brochures defining primary care and giving instructions on how to access the new system. Business cards were developed to be handed out by the primary care provider to introduce the patient to his/her primary care provider and team. All educational materials were color-coded by group. All patient educational materials produced were approved by the chair of the Medical Center Patient Education Committee and the Primary Care Planning/Implementation Group. Clinical staff were asked to discuss the anticipated changes with the patients they were currently seeing and to give them a pamphlet about the initiation of primary care.

While educating patients about primary care, it was also necessary to educate them about the importance of preventive health and other aspects of general patient education as part of our commitment to the primary care concept. The subgroup proposed a dedicated Patient Education Center where handouts, videos, and personal computers were available and state-of-the-art learning could take place. Space and budget had to be identified to support the center.

Space Subgroup   The space subgroup worked on a major stumbling block—allocating appropriate space to meet the goals of primary care. However, as inpatient wards were closing due to the move to ambulatory care, space became available for clinics. Engineering Service worked closely with the clinical staff to create temporary exam rooms for the clinics; later, more permanent space was created. For example, when the Neurology Service closed one of two 30-bed wards, it was able to locate its clinic and remaining inpatient ward side by side, an ideal solution for both staff and patients. Laboratory and radiology support for primary care was crucial, so space for them was chosen close to the clinic areas.

Informatics Subgroup   The informatics subgroup identified needed information systems. Because primary care required an increased availability of information, software to support this need had to be created. However, the difficulty in developing new information systems to tap appropriate data was underestimated. Scheduling packages had to be adapted to allow one hour for an initial evaluation and 15 to 30 minutes for follow-up visits. Patients had to be identified in the computer by group color and primary care provider. Panels of patients for the individual providers needed to be established. The VA Decentralized Hospital Computer Program provided an electronic health summary on every patient. However, an electronic system for consults also needed to be developed, as did software to support provider profile information and to track and trend data. Problems arose because there was a need for the development of specific clinical indicators and a core database compatible with other databases. Solutions to these problems required an inordinate amount of time and effort by the Primary Care Planning/Implementation Group, the Nursing Informatics coordinator, and the Information Management Service.

Evaluation Subgroup   The evaluation subgroup developed the primary care implementation monitors. Criteria were selected based on the objectives of the project and the availability of data sources. Monitors revolved around the patient database, quality assurance (QA), and productivity measures. QA monitors included length of stay, polypharmacy, admissions within three days following a primary care clinic visit, and satisfaction within groups of customers. Productivity measures included number of visits per patient per year, Ambulatory Evaluation Clinic (AEC) utilization, next available appointment, wait times in the clinics, frequency of consultation requests, and wait time in the AEC.

Progress and Changes during Transition/Implementation

Table 2-1 shows some key events during the transition and implementation phases.

While in the transition/implementation phase, several major changes occurred that influenced the original planning. First, the medical center director was reassigned to another VAMC in July 1994. In August, the new acting director, who supported the planning for a new care delivery model, started monitoring patient wait times in AEC. The clinicians set a standard that patients would wait no longer than two hours before being seen in the AEC. To meet this goal, the chief of medicine and nurse executive moved the start date for Urgent Care Clinic (walk-in) functions from July 1995 to December 1994. With less than a month's preparation time, staffing needed to be rearranged, competencies verified, and information systems put in place. Urgent care was implemented on December 3, 1994. Following this initiation of the Urgent Care Clinic, the nurse executive arranged a pizza party for all staff to celebrate a major milestone and to recognize staff who were responsible for implementing the changes.

A second major change occurred in October 1994 when the acting director elevated the nurse executive position to associate director for patient services, making her responsible for four direct-care services in addition to nursing. Even though the clinical bed services and nursing were working well together, there was no coordination with the other support services (that is, social work, nutrition, and pharmacy). Also, there had been no mandate or direction for those services to support the movement toward primary care. With the change in administrative structure, social work, nutrition, pharmacy, and audiology services began reporting to the associate director for patient services in January 1995. The vision of interdisciplinary self-directed work teams became a reality as

Table 2-1. Milestones in the Transition and Implementation Phases

Date	Primary Care Implementation Events
March 1994	• Patient groups identified and criteria for patient placement developed • Retraining of all staff physicians and nurse practitioners initiated • Patient education begun
October	• Resources redistributed from inpatient to outpatient services • Unions involved • Nurse executive elevated to associate director for patient services
December	• Urgent care primary clinics established
January 1995	• Telephone Medical Advice Line established • Social work, pharmacy, and nutrition and food reassigned to the associate director for patient services; interdisciplinary teams identified
June	• Each inpatient ward coupled with an outpatient clinic
July	• Primary care fully implemented—outpatient and inpatient
January 1996	• Evaluation and continuous monitoring/improvement
January 1997	• Preventive medicine efforts fully established

she now was able to influence the chiefs of those services to reorganize along the same lines as nursing. This ensured that all staff would be assigned to an interdisciplinary primary care team that supported both outpatient and inpatient care. These services quickly came on board, and an interdisciplinary patient services team was established to support each of the four general medical groups: neurology, psychiatry, geriatrics, and extended care.

The associate director for patient services viewed this as an opportunity to begin changing the culture of the medical center by helping those services that directly support patient care to begin working together, thus establishing one culture and one approach to patient care. Nurses were asked to share their expertise, knowledge, and resources by including social workers, dietitians, and pharmacists in their classes and meetings on primary care. Staffs who rarely talked to one another were now planning together. The elevation of the nurse executive position greatly facilitated this approach. The newly organized patient services were glad to be a part of the major change about to occur in the medical center and began eagerly to support this redesign of patient care.

The impact of this role change was positive in other ways. Because the associate director for patient services reported directly to the medical center director and was a member of senior administration, she guaranteed that all changes supported high-quality patient care and sound management. For example, in the late spring of 1995, when it was suggested that there be a pilot of only one group rather than implementation of the full model as planned, she was able to persuade the Primary Care Planning/Implementation Group that a pilot of only one group would be extremely confusing and complicate the process even more. Because she had a passion for the primary care model and its impact on patient care, she was able to guide and support all staff, some of whom were having difficulty with the vision and changes associated with primary care.

With urgent care in place in December 1994, it was decided to start the Medical Advice Line in January 1995, since this was a cornerstone for primary care and supported the standard of no more than two-hour waits in AEC. Again, with only a month's preparation, staff needed to be recruited and protocol/algorithms developed. A software package from a West Coast VAMC was imported, piloted, and programmed to meet our needs. The assistant chief of medicine for ambulatory care became clinically responsible for this program and approved all protocols. The RNs assigned to the program were heavily involved in patient education and communication with the primary care providers. Also, many calls were received regarding veteran eligibility and clinic appointments; therefore, a clerk was added to the staff to manage these calls.

Other changes occurred during implementation that affected the objective of primary care being a budget-neutral project. Existing resources needed to be redirected as new programs were implemented (such as the Medical Advice Line, patient education, and the preadmission program to support primary care). It was anticipated that there would be no increase in FTEs, and that the medical center would go through some downsizing during this transition. However, the enormity of the process was unanticipated. To remain competitive and meet the national VA performance standards to decrease bed days of care and lengths of stay, the center needed to close beds and wards. Each time there was a closure, there was an FTE decrease in nursing, and, to a lesser degree, in other patient services. RIFs were not required because new FTE levels could be reached through attrition. However, this meant staff who remained needed to be assigned wherever vacancies were occurring. Frequently, psychiatry nurses found themselves on medical-surgical units, and medical-surgical nurses were now spending more time in the clinic areas. In addition, most of the workload moved to the ambulatory setting, and care that used to be provided to inpatients was now being done on an outpatient basis (for example, wound care, diabetic teaching, blood transfusions, and so on). This created an increased burden on nursing educational staff for teaching and verifying new required competencies.

Key Players

As with all successful projects, there are usually some "stars" that emerge to light things up. The RN project coordinator, though well chosen, was better than anyone could have imagined. Her enthusiasm about her assignment showed in the quality of her work. Her interpersonal skills just kept getting better and better, thus ensuring successful outcomes. She and the assistant chief of medicine for ambulatory care became a dynamic duo. They spoke with one voice, making it easier for the Primary Care Planning/Implementation Group to reach consensus on issues and problems.

The nursing informatics coordinator's clinical background enabled her to bridge the gap between what the clinicians needed and what the technical experts could produce. The chair of the Patient Education Committee, a nurse, was invaluable in preparing patients for the changes. And totally unexpected was the support and understanding received from the CFO. It was delightful to receive his administrative input, but even more so to listen to his "patient perspective." He was able to speak fluently to others in the medical center about the primary care model and the advantages to patient care.

Evaluation Phase

Evaluation was designed around the original objectives: to implement a primary care model that identified patient groups and provided care that was competent, accessible, continuous, and comprehensive. Additional objectives were to provide each patient with a health care provider that he or she would know and who would provide continuity of care in a cost-efficient and budget-neutral manner.

Evaluation showed the model distributed patients into seven different primary care groups with a primary care provider for each patient. This change allowed each patient to begin to identify with his/her own care group and provider. The model also decreased the random movement of patients from clinic to clinic and permitted the primary care provider to give continuous care. These results have been verified in a survey of patients. [15–18]

Outpatient Survey Results

An outpatient satisfaction survey was used to investigate patient perception of outcomes. It was given to each primary care group of patients (n = 115 in each primary care group) in 1995, 1996, and 1997, and addressed standards such as quality of care, provision of health care information and education, preference in decisions concerning health care, emotional support, coordination of care, one provider of care, and timely access to health care. When the results from early 1997 were compared to those from 1995 and 1996, the scores indicated continuous improvement in all but one indicator. The overall patient satisfaction with quality of care increased 13 percent from 1995 to 1997. Satisfaction with provision of health care information and education increased 10 percent, indicating that the goal of including wellness and prevention as part of comprehensive care is starting to succeed. The patients' satisfaction concerning their involvement and preference in decisions concerning their health care also increased 10 percent from 1995 to 1997. Satisfaction with coordination of care increased 15 percent. The patients' response to questions that addressed the provision of care by one provider increased 23 percent. Satisfaction with timely access to care has not changed appreciably; however, it was already at the 85 percent level. [19–22]

Another process to improve timeliness of care was the effort to decrease wait times in the AEC and for appointments to clinics. In 1994, 49 percent of patients waited longer than two hours to be seen in AEC. By 1997, wait times had decreased dramatically, with 93 percent of the patients waiting less than two hours.[23] In 1994, some specialty clinics had 60-day wait times for clinic appointments; in 1997, the time for the next available appointment in all primary clinics was less than seven days.[24-29]

Other indicators of success included increased outpatient activities, decreased bed days of care, and decreased average length of stay (ALOS). In 1994, there were a total of 214,419 clinic visits, with 341,420 encounters for care.[30,31] In 1997 there were 331,469 clinic visits with 489,417 encounters for care.[32] During that same time frame bed days of care decreased from 147,515 in 1994 to 57,419 in 1997.[33] The ALOS decreased almost 45 percent.[34] These savings allow a decrease in the cost of providing care per patient while providing more comprehensive care to an additional 2,748 new veteran patients.

Another indicator of success was meeting and exceeding the goal of budget neutrality at a time when there was no increase in the medical center budget, due to a congressional directive preventing the usual and expected increases to account for inflation. This model was also implemented while remaining more than competitive with other VA medical centers of like size and complexity in regard to nursing service FTE costs and patient care costs.

Unanticipated Outcomes

Like all large projects, some unanticipated outcomes occurred. One such outcome was an increase in pharmacy costs and in the number of prescriptions rather than the expected decrease due to a more coordinated care approach. Although not fully explored, the explanation for the unexpected cost increase may lie in more rigorous attention to all pharmacy costs required by the associate director for patient services, an increase in the number of veterans served, and the increased cost of mailing many more prescriptions associated with our growing outpatient population. As this cost increase came to the attention of the associate director for patient services, some interventions were planned, which included a literature search that indicated this was not unexpected with the initial implementation of primary care. In 1997, there was a downward trend in pharmacy costs, possibly the result of assigning a specific pharmacist to each primary team to work with physicians.

Another unanticipated outcome was the continued long wait time to the next appointment in the specialty clinics, as was the reluctance of some specialists to transfer patients from the specialty and subspecialty clinics to primary care. For those physicians who requested assistance, nurses were assigned to the specialty clinics to explain the advantages of having a single primary care provider and to enroll patients in the appropriate primary care group. This maneuver helped decrease the long wait times for clinic appointments and helped assign patients to the proper primary care group. Also, efficiency of care was increased when the specialist physicians developed practice guidelines to assist the primary care providers to manage patients in the primary care clinics rather than referring them to the specialty clinics.

Implementing primary care in a highly affiliated academic setting has been more difficult than expected because of the high rotation rate of residents, interns, and medical students who needed to be educated about their role. This also affected efforts to educate patients about their primary care providers. To help resolve this, work continues with the universities to plan rotations that permit residents to follow an identified patient population throughout their training program.

Major Successes

One major success was the impact of nurses and nursing across the medical center. Because of the nurse executive's reputation as a leader and team player before the transition to primary care, she was able to establish the importance of nursing to the change process. Her power base had long been established in the medical center and, indeed, throughout the VA system. She perceived her position to be one of authority and responsibility. She had always practiced recognized management principles that contributed to her reputation as a leader. She was known for her ability to recognize the big picture, to be non-parochial about nursing service, and to work collaboratively with other services and organizations.

Her vision of the importance of nursing was evidenced by the intense nurse involvement at all levels of planning and implementation, as well as the ready acceptance of nurses as co-leaders of the primary care groups. As primary care co-leaders, nurses are responsible for managing high-quality and cost-effective care for a specified group of patients, as well as for facilitating the integration of all disciplines into patient-focused, self-directed work teams.

The elevation of the nurse executive to a patient care executive was viewed as another success, because it was the beginning of an organizational culture change. It was also a validation of the view that patient care services are the core business of the medical center. Clinical leaders are now working together effectively to ensure organizational success and facilitate the integration of patient care across service lines. The advent of this model demonstrated that continuous and seamless care could be provided by a designated team. As staff have had the opportunity to present lectures and distribute posters, the strengths and uniqueness of our model are becoming recognized. The staff are frequently sought as consultants, particularly regarding implementation of the inpatient-outpatient aspects of the model. Also, other VAMCs are becoming interested in neurology and psychiatry primary care groups.

Lessons Learned

There were many lessons learned in this transition. One was the importance of committed leadership as well as a committed full-time project coordinator. The proper selection of these persons was crucial to success. We also learned that the lag time between implementation and expected changes can be longer than planned. Experience showed that the interdisciplinary team could be depended on to accomplish far more than expected when the chips were down. Our initial perception was verified that it would be difficult to change from an existing, comfortable style of practice to the new model; however, the model is in place and staff have accepted the change and are moving ahead. Our belief was confirmed that it was extremely important for all clinical personnel to work together and to have the same vision of primary patient care. We found that implementation required constant attention to details, readjustments as needed, and a constant review of quality of care. Finally, we learned to expect the unexpected.

There are some things we would do differently if we had the opportunity. Additional research on self-directed work teams would have been helpful; we might have been able to work through the process of team development with less frustration. Along with this, it would have helped to start training staff sooner on how to work at the interdisciplinary team level and how to build consensus. These were some of the most difficult concepts to put into practice, but they were essential. It would have been beneficial to have the roles of the service chiefs and primary care co-leaders more clearly defined before actually starting. The chiefs of patient services were somewhat concerned about their changing management role and the requirement to move to a new and different leadership style. They needed guidance in developing the skills of transformational leadership.

There are some things we would *not* change because they work well and are right for the veteran and the medical center. First, we would not change the primary care model—its strengths far outweigh any weaknesses encountered so far. Second, weekly meetings for planning, problem solving, and implementation review were an ideal method of resolving issues and enabled the project to move ahead on target. Furthermore, nursing and other patient services placed high value on the opportunities to work closely with physicians across the medical center.

Conclusion

This case study presents one example of patient care redesign. The traditional system of highly specialized, multiple caregivers was replaced with a single primary care provider and an interdisciplinary team. Care now is coordinated and comprehensive rather than episodic, fragmented, and reactive. Interdisciplinary collaborative relationships have replaced the old independent service relationships. Inpatient care is now replaced with a model that is outpatient/inpatient oriented. Staff formerly assigned either to a ward or clinic are now assigned to both ward and clinical functions. Primary care groups are co-led by the two professionals most responsible for patient care, a master's-prepared RN and a physician. Patients no longer consult with a cast of thousands but see the same team members, whether in the clinic or on the ward. The model was successfully implemented not only in a budget-neutral fashion but also in a budget-reduction environment that affected patient care funding for all VA medical centers. In conclusion, this large tertiary care medical center has made the transition to a primary care delivery model while maintaining clinical, research, and educational missions.

References

1. Department of Veterans Affairs, *Inpatient Statistical Summary 1994* (Austin, TX: Austin Automated Center, 1994).

2. Department of Veterans Affairs, *Coin Ops Report 1994* (Austin, TX: Austin Automated Center, 1994).

3. Washington VA Medical Center, *Nursing Service Strength Report 1994* (Washington, DC: VAMC, 1994).

4. Veterans Affairs Central Office, *Managed Care Strategy,* report (Washington, DC:VHA Managed Health Care Task Force, 1993).

5. S. Allcorn, *Using Matrix Organization to Manage Health Care Delivery Organizations,* reprint, Administrator, Department of Medicine, Box Med, 601 (Rochester, NY: University of Rochester, 1993).

6. E. S. Fisher and G. H. Welch, *Reform Options for the Department of Veterans Affairs,* presented at Primary Care Conference, Eastern Region RMEC, Department of Veterans Affairs, December 1, 1993.

7. T. Parrino, *Productivity Measurement and Quality Improvement in Primary Care,* presented at Primary Care Conference, Eastern Region RMEC, Department of Veterans Affairs, November 30, 1993.

8. R. P. Mogielnicki, *White River Junction VA and the Vermont Reform Process: A Work in Progress,* presented at Primary Care Conference, Eastern Region RMEC, Department of Veterans Affairs, December 1, 1993.

9. L. B. Burnes Bolton, C. Aydin, G. Popolow, and J. Ramseyer, "Ten Steps for Managing Organization Change," *JONA* 22, no. 6 (1992): 14–20.

10. L. B. Burnes Bolton, G. Poplow, J. Ramseyer, and C. Aydin, *PATH: Planning Alliance for Tomorrow's Health Care,* poster presentation at American Association of Nurse Executives (AONE) Annual Conference, May 1991, San Diego, CA.

11. J. A. Rizzo, M. P. Gilman, and C. A. Mersmann, "Facilitating Care Delivery Redesign Using Measure of Unit Culture and Work Characteristics, *JONA* 24, no. 5 (1994): 32–37.

12. J. Bostrom and J. Zimmerman, "Restructuring Nursing for a Competitive Health Care Environment," *Nursing Economic$* 11, no. 1 (1993): 35–54.

13. M. Hammer and J. Champy, *Reengineering the Corporation: A Manifesto for Business Revolution* (New York: Harper Business, 1993).

14. Veterans Affairs Central Office, *VHA Directive 10-94-100 Oct. 1994,* Washington, DC, 1994.

15. Washington VA Medical Center, *Performance Report 1995* (Washington, DC: Office of Quality Management, 1995).

16. Washington VA Medical Center, *Performance Report FY '96* (Washington, DC: Office of Planning, Education, and Performance Improvement, 1996).

17. Washington VA Medical Center, *Outpatient Satisfaction Survey: Medical Primary Care Clinics* (Washington, DC: Office of Planning, Education, and Performance Improvement, February 1997).

18. Washington VA Medical Center, *Outpatient Satisfaction Survey: Geriatric Primary Care Clinic* (Washington, DC: Office of Planning, Education, and Performance Improvement, April 1997).

19. Washington VA Medical Center, *Performance Report 1995* (Washington, DC: Office of Quality Management, 1995).

20. Washington VA Medical Center, *Performance Report FY '96* (Washington, DC: Office of Planning, Education, and Performance Improvement, April 1997).

21. Washington VA Medical Center, *Outpatient Satisfaction Survey: Medical Primary Care Clinics* (Washington, DC: Office of Planning, Education, and Performance Improvement, February 1997).

22. Washington VA Medical Center, *Outpatient Satisfaction Survey: Geriatric Primary Care Clinic* (Washington, DC: Office of Planning, Education, and Performance Improvement, April 1997).

23. Washington VA Medical Center, *AEC Waiting-Time Study,* QA Monitor Report, VAMC Washington, DC, 1997.

24. Washington VA Medical Center, *Performance Report 1995* (Washington, DC: Office of Quality Management, 1995).

25. Washington VA Medical Center, *Performance Report FY '96* (Washington, DC: Office of Planning, Education, and Performance Improvement, 1996).

26. Washington VA Medical Center, *Outpatient Satisfaction Survey: Medical Primary Care Clinics* (Washington, DC: Office of Planning, Education, and Performance Improvement, February 1997).

27. Washington VA Medical Center, *Outpatient Satisfaction Survey: Geriatric Primary Care Clinic* (Washington, DC: Office of Planning, Education, and Performance Improvement, April 1997).

28. Washington VA Medical Center, *AEC Waiting-Time Study,* QA Monitor Report, VAMC Washington, DC, 1997.

29. Veterans Affairs Central Office, *Quality Improvement Check List (QUIC) Report for 1994,* Washington, DC, 1994.

30. Department of Veterans Affairs, *Coin Ops Report 1994* (Austin, TX: Austin Automated Center, 1994).

31. VHA National Customer Feedback Center, "Performance on Customer Service Standards: Recently Discharged Inpatients," 1994 Survey Report (Washington, DC: VAMC West Roxbury, MA, 1994).

32. Washington VA Medical Center, *Weekly Performance Report 1997* (Washington, DC: Office of Planning, Education, and Quality Improvement, 1997).

33. Ibid.

34. Veterans Health Administration, *1997 Network Performance Agreement Report VISN 5 Bed Days of Care* (Durham, NC: National Performance Data Resource Center, 1997).

CHAPTER THREE

Restructuring to Provide Synergistic Patient Care

Peggy A. Haggerty, RN, MSN
Mary Lu Gerke, RN, MSN

Gundersen Lutheran is a 350-bed, acute care teaching hospital/ clinic located in La Crosse, Wisconsin. Its nursing department began decentralization in the late 1970s. Although not realized at the time, decentralization laid the foundation on which to explore and create a new patient-centered delivery model for Gundersen Lutheran—the differentiated practice model. This case study describes the model and discusses its benefits and some of the problems encountered during its implementation phase. It also describes how some of the nursing roles at Gundersen Lutheran changed in response to this particular approach to patient-centered care.

Impetus for Change

Although this country has experienced cycles of nursing short-ages, the 1980s brought a different type of shortage. National nursing leaders restated the problem, describing it as a "short-age of professional nursing" rather than a nursing shortage. The environment was ripe to reassess what staff member was doing what and why. The nursing culture of Gundersen Lutheran had strengthened and matured into a fertile ground for change, where the change agent was the staff at the bedside. Focusing on the need to move to a higher level of patient care, Gundersen began a restructuring effort.

In *Leadership and the New Science,* Wheatley describes organizational vision as an energy field, "a force of unseen connections that influence employees' behavior—rather than as an evocative message about some desired future state."[1] The vice president of nursing at Gundersen Lutheran engaged an energy field of sorts in her vision for the nursing department. She envisioned nursing in a partnership role with patients in the delivery of their care. Her vision moved well beyond the nursing department and developed into an organizationwide patient-driven care delivery model.

Differentiated Practice Model

This practice model involves differentiating traditional roles within the hospital setting to make patient care delivery both more efficient and more personal. It began with the differentiation of the registered nurse (RN) roles, then led to the examination and redesign of other patient support roles. The following subsections describe implementation of this model at Gundersen Lutheran in three stages:

1. Creation of the case manager and case associate nursing roles
2. Creation of the patient service assistant (PSA) position
3. Implementation of a pilot PSA program

Phase 1. Studying the Professional Nurse Role

The first phase in redesign efforts began in 1988 with a study of the role of the professional nurse. The nursing model in place was the primary nursing model, successful in some patient care areas and given lip service in others. Because the nurse was the professional at the patient's side 24 hours a day, it was hoped that nursing leadership and staff could develop a new role for nursing that would release the creative energy to build a new patient care delivery model that would take Gundersen Lutheran into the twenty-first century.

A task force of RNs from each unit, several nursing directors, the quality assurance director, and the vice president of nursing decided to work with a consultant to assess the structure and functions of the current primary nursing model. The motivation to perform this assessment was not related to a nursing shortage but, rather, a misuse of nursing services. It was driven by the recognition that patients' needs and expectations and economic factors were changing. It had become evident that Gundersen Lutheran was not using professional nurses in a way that capitalized on their educational and nursing competencies. "With health, human response, and quality of life as new imperatives to integrate into each individual's care, the way in which nursing care was organized and delivered clearly required a fundamental change."[2] The nurses' task force developed the following plan:

- Create a multidisciplinary patient care team to promote a seamless delivery system.
- Move services closer to the patient and ensure patient-driven structures.
- Improve and enhance the physical environment to support patient-driven care.
- Eliminate duplication of existing roles to increase efficiency and cost-effectiveness.
- Increase patient and staff satisfaction.
- Develop ways to attract and retain nursing professionals.

Often, when confusion abounded, these principles would be used to keep the task force on track so that members could focus on the main purpose and thrust of the work.

The task force used the work of two projects—Facilitating ADN Competency Development and Defining, and Differentiating ADN and BSN Competencies, sponsored by the

Midwest Alliance in Nursing (MAIN) and funded by the W. K. Kellogg Foundation—to help design a differentiated nursing model. These projects were researched and developed between 1980 and 1984.[3] The underlying belief of the differentiated nursing model is that "each nurse is expert in his/her role, each role is mutually valued, and collaborative practice utilizing both roles is the whole of nursing."[4]

Redesigning the Professional Nursing Framework Differentiating nursing roles meant redesigning the professional nursing framework. The vice president of patient services set the vision and formed a decentralized team of grassroots nursing staff, which fully participated in every step of planning and implementing the new model. Koerner and Karpiuk explain the importance of culture when implementing major change. "Culture is a paradox: it has the capacity stubbornly to resist change or creatively, and even ingeniously, to embrace it."[5]

The staff embraced the work and developed professional nursing job descriptions and performance appraisals for two roles: the case manager and the case associate. The *case manager* role was designed to be accountable for the independent scope of practice and focused on health and human response. The *case associate* role was designed to be accountable for the dependent scope of nursing practice and focused on the technical aspects of care. Together, they were designed to deliver the full scope of nursing practice to each individual. The roles were based on RN competencies, thereby allowing all currently employed RNs, regardless of educational background, to be eligible for either role. Later, the professional RN roles were defined more clearly and now a baccalaureate is required for any new care manager hired from outside the hospital.

Implementing the New Model The research, discussions, and numerous drafts for the differentiated practice model were concluded in mid-1989, and the real test was to present the proposed roles to all staff and develop an implementation plan.

All professional staff were required to take a minimum of eight hours of education on the differentiated nursing model. After they had grasped the basis of the model, they were asked to complete a factoring tool. The tool assisted practicing nurses in discovering the competencies they excelled at and preferred. Then each staff nurse met with the director of his or her unit to decide whether these competencies made them more suitable to the case manager or the case associate role. A one-year commitment was made, after which nurses could choose to change roles. Case managers attended 16 hours of education, and case associates participated in 8 hours of education. Before implementation in early 1990, physicians, other departmental personnel, and the board of directors were also offered education on the new nursing model.

In retrospect, we believe training the case associates and case managers together would have contributed to their mutual understanding and valuing each others' roles from the start. At the time, however, it seemed that case managers would require more education related to the expanded responsibilities and accountabilities of the role as well as new expectations of care planning across the continuum. However, we later realized the case associate role was also new and different. We learned that no matter how well one plans for the education in a new model, improvements are almost always needed. Recognizing this has helped us in our educational planning with subsequent redesign efforts.

The new model was implemented on all acute care nursing units. Consideration was given to the fact that various patient populations' needs required different numbers of case associates and case managers. Through trial and error, each unit determined the appropriate mix based on the following factors:

- The amount of collaborative patient care activity taking place on the unit
- Degree of acuity on the unit
- Numbers of daily admissions and discharges
- Amount of discharge planning needed

For the critical care units, one or two case managers worked best, while for a 30-bed surgical unit, eight or ten case managers were more appropriate.

Each unit established a practice committee whose function was to address issues and solve problems. Initially, the model implemented was based on the outside consultant's recommendation that the case manager be given both patient assignments for direct care and case management responsibilities. Because the goal was for every patient to have a case manager, it soon became apparent that case managers did not have time to give direct patient care and also meet the expectations and responsibilities of case management.

The rehab unit was the first unit to completely differentiate the case manager and case associate roles by pulling the case manager out of direct patient care. It redefined the number of case managers needed to serve all the patients on the unit, which led to the factoring tool being revised and all nursing staff being refactored. As a result, job descriptions were changed to reflect further differentiation of the case manager and case associate roles. Because case managers were no longer given patient assignments for care, case associates were assigned more patients, with a licensed practical nurse (LPN) or nursing assistant to attend to the daily care of the patients. This freed case managers to tend to individualized care planning for patients. Efficiency and effectiveness were gained through the case managers being able to concentrate on the coordination of patient care, resulting in a budget-neutral outcome.

With this change, further education was needed in the areas of delegation and teamwork. Workshops and in-service training dealing with these two elements were set up to support and promote the work of the two roles. Trust and respect for each other's work became the basis for successfully meeting the needs of patients and families.

Gundersen Lutheran has had a high retention rate for a number of years. With implementation of the differentiated practice model, RN turnover rates have remained below 5 percent, leading us to believe that the professional staff is satisfied with the changes that have occurred. Surveys have reflected both staff and patient satisfaction with the new model of care delivery.

Phase 2. Decentralizing the Ancillary Roles

As the differentiated RN roles were implemented, feedback began coming in from the nursing staff:

- They believed that other departments did not understand patient-driven care.
- Case managers often felt there was a lack of cooperation and a narrow focus by nonnursing departments.
- There seemed to be no one to whom to delegate some of the nonnursing tasks.
- The nursing assistant could not be fully utilized in a direct-care role while being responsible for nonnursing tasks (such as cleaning dirty utensils and stocking supplies for the unit).

What became evident was the effect that the change in nursing practice had on the whole organizational system. Differentiating nursing roles resulted in a change of professional nursing practice, making more evident the tasks and responsibilities that could be done by others. Focus needed to turn to the support functions available to the professional nurse, which prompted the second phase of redesign.

The second phase of redesign involved looking at how the organization could enhance patient care while providing job satisfaction and enrichment for those delivering patient services. It was decided to develop a hospitality role to enhance the caring component of services to patients. According to Doerge and Hagenow, caring is the major focus of nursing. This concept needs to be integrated at every level—within ourselves, our relationships, and in our organizations—to make a difference.[6] Continuity of care and bringing services closer to the patient through cross-training efforts were key in our redesign efforts.

Creation of the Patient Service Assistant Position   In 1991, the vice president of nursing again formed a task force, this time a multidisciplinary committee with representation from nursing, housekeeping, environmental services, laundry, patient services, nutrition services, respiratory care, volunteer services, management systems, and administration. It met in a brainstorming session to look at what the optimal customer-service delivery would be on the patient care unit as provided by ancillary staff, including how to provide hotel-like services in a hospital setting. Over the next year, the ideas generated in this session were refined and incorporated by the multidisciplinary committee into a workable job description initially called a hospitality associate and now called a patient service assistant.

PSAs were given two areas of responsibility: environmental (cleaning of patient rooms and physical support spaces) and hospitality (comfort and care provided to patients through environmental support services). The reason for developing this particular role was to eliminate existing duplication of roles, increase efficiency and cost-effectiveness, expand teamwork to provide support services for the direct-care workers, move services closer to the patient, and increase patient and staff satisfaction.

In determining how to eliminate existing duplication of roles, it was necessary to evaluate how the work was being done currently. It was found that preparing a patient's room for a new admission involved three different types of workers from three different departments reporting to their respective department heads. This was a multiple-step process that often resulted in delays in room assignments. The three types of workers involved in the process were:

- *Housekeepers:* The housekeepers reported to the department head of Environmental Services, a centralized department. Most of the employees were full-time and assigned to clean patient rooms and the patient care areas, primarily on the day shift. Usually, there were one or two assigned to a unit.

- *Unit makers:* The unit makers made up a centralized department that reported to the Patient Services Department head. They floated throughout the hospital, washing down beds and applying clean linens after patients were discharged.
- *Nursing assistants:* Nursing assistants were decentralized to the patient care unit and reported directly to the nurse manager of that unit. Their responsibilities at that time were mainly indirect patient care, which involved stripping the patient room after the patient was discharged, cleaning dirty utensils, and stocking the unit. A small amount of their time was spent in direct care by assisting staff with patients' daily living activities.

The steps involved in the process of preparing a room for a new admission were as follows:

1. Nursing assistant strips the room of dirty linen and equipment.
2. Housekeeper mops, dusts, and cleans the room.
3. Unit maker is paged to finish the room.

The process was not very efficient. The room might not be a top priority for the housekeeper on the unit, based on what she had to do at the time. There was lag time from the time the unit makers were paged until their arrival on the floor, based on their priorities. According to Strasen, there is a 40 percent downtime spent by centralized departments traveling to and from patient care areas to provide services.[7] If the patient left after the usual hours for housekeepers and unit makers, the room would have to be cleaned by nursing staff or left until the next day, depending on need.

The PSA role became a combination of these three job functions and new responsibilities that focused on customer service and hospitality. These new responsibilities included welcoming and orienting patients to their rooms, helping them put away their belongings, and providing any necessary supplies. In addition, the PSA assisted staff in the delivery of meal trays, getting water for patients, answering lights, transporting patients at time of discharge, and stocking the unit with supplies.

Opposition to the PSA Position The multidisciplinary committee was very active in finalizing a job description, seeking input from the various staffs representing housekeeping, patient services, and nursing. However, a major obstacle was a lack of buy-in from the housekeepers and unit makers not on the committee. They felt threatened, knowing that the new role would be changing how they did their work and with whom they would be working. In addition, they felt the new job description was overwhelming, and they were anxious about taking on responsibility for providing indirect care to patients. Previously, they had been expected to do their work quickly and not spend time talking with patients; now, they would be required to welcome patients and be responsible for communicating any concerns to the RNs. Also, the PSAs would be decentralized to the patient care unit and become part of that unit's staffing pattern and patient care team. Another threat was the change in lifestyle necessitated by having to work shifts based on patient activity, which meant many would need to work rotating shifts. Focusing on a patient-driven system versus a task-driven system was a paradigmatic shift for this group of workers.

Another major issue the committee had to address was the fact that the housekeepers, unit makers, and nursing assistants were in a collective bargaining unit. It was imperative to have a leader from the bargaining unit at the table. This individual supported the new PSA position but often challenged the committee as the job description was being developed to ensure that no duties of the position would be done by any other, nonunionized employee. Also, the collective bargaining unit feared that union positions would be eliminated by the new role. The committee reassured the collective bargaining unit that this was not the intent, but rather that it was to improve patient care by enhancing the jobs of those currently in the affected union positions. This link with the union proved to be a key element in communicating the committee's interpretation of the new job to union members. The vice president of nursing worked closely with the collective bargaining unit's leadership, keeping them abreast of the committee's work throughout the process.

Phase 3. Implementing the Pilot Plan

A pilot PSA program was planned for the Orthopedics/ Gynecology Unit and scheduled to begin in August 1992 and run through April of 1993. After plans for the pilot were finalized by the interdisciplinary committee and presurveys of patient and staff satisfaction were distributed, formal informational sessions were set up in July 1992 for the housekeepers, unit makers, and nursing assistants. This was to present an overview of the work that had been done by the committee, the objectives of the program, and the plan for implementing the pilot.

Positions were posted for the new PSA role with the hope of attracting current housekeepers, unit makers, and nursing assistants. However, there proved to be little interest among current employees, and only a few applied. There was a "wait-and-see" attitude; some hoped the pilot would fail and the program would go away and allow them to continue in their current roles. Interviewing and hiring for the new positions were done jointly by the department head of Environmental Services and the nurse manager of the Orthopedic/Gynecology Unit.

When the PSA roles for the pilot were filled, formal educational sessions were set up by the Human Resources Development Department. These focused on communication as it related to customer service, housekeeping responsibilities, unit makers' responsibilities, and the components of the nursing assistant responsibilities that would be transferred to the new job. Participation by housekeepers, unit makers, and nursing assistants in the cross-education of those individuals hired in PSA positions occurred. In addition, formal orientation days were scheduled on the pilot unit to familiarize the new PSAs with the unit, the location of equipment, and the organization and routines of the different shifts.

The PSAs were decentralized to the patient care unit and reported jointly to the nurse manager and the director of Environmental Services. That reporting structure changed shortly after implementation to reporting only to the nurse manager, to avoid confusion as to whom the PSA should consult for requests and problem solving. The mechanism for receiving updates on environmental cleaning standards remained in place for the PSAs. A small group of housekeepers would be retained as part of the centralized Environmental Services Department to clean the nonpatient care areas.

In January 1993, postimplementation patient and staff satisfaction surveys were distributed. Results for patient satisfaction revealed very positive responses to both the pre- and postsurvey questions. Staff satisfaction also revealed no major changes; however, unit makers responded less favorably overall, particularly to questions related to change. This was believed to be the result of changes in their role after the PSA pilot was implemented.

Benefits of Pilot Plan Implementation With implementation of the PSA role, efficiencies were gained in many areas, including terminal bed cleaning. Previously, a number of steps had been involved in preparing a discharged room for a new admission, with delays due to travel time and competing priorities. Now, PSAs are present on the unit when patients are discharged and able to complete tasks that once involved three different departments. This has resulted in a quicker turnover of patient rooms and very few delays for the patients.

In addition, implementation of the new PSA role resulted in a redistribution of full-time-equivalent (FTE) employees. Time studies were conducted for the tasks performed by the housekeepers, unit makers, and nursing assistants related to indirect care to establish the number of FTEs needed in the PSA role. These studies also enabled us to determine how many FTEs were needed from the Environmental Services Department, Patient Services, and Nursing. This meant patient care units would need to adjust their staffing patterns and balance them based on the FTEs that were given to the PSA role by the nursing assistant's indirect patient care tasks. The goal was to be budget neutral.

Another benefit of the role redesign was that decentralization moved the work closer to the patient, which had the effect of producing a more patient-centered approach to care. We were able to provide coverage over a greater span of time than was possible previously. Before the PSA program, the housekeepers worked from 7:00 A.M. to 3:00 P.M. Currently, patient care units are staffed based on the patient activity of the unit, anywhere from 8 to 24 hours a day. Therefore, a nursing assistant is available to assist staff with the direct care of patients for a longer period of time.

Yet another benefit is that job satisfaction is high among PSAs. They feel part of the team, are involved in helping meet patient needs, and are accountable to patients, staff, and the patient care units. Often they are ahead of the staff in organizing their work, so they are available to assist with discharges, room changes, stocking the unit, and so on.

In addition, other departments better understand what patient-driven care is and how ancillary departments are integral to its efficient functioning. Moreover, collaboration and communication have improved among the various roles and departments. New relationships have formed. Doerge and Hagenow state it best when they say that "relationships are the basis for teams, partnerships, and alliances which influence our organizations."[8]

The goal was to have the PSA program implemented hospitalwide by the end of the pilot program. However, this did not occur because the labor contract had to be negotiated and the revised job classifications approved. Once that happened, implementation phases began in August 1994 and were completed by the end of September. In the meantime, the program continued on the Orthopedics/Gynecology Unit. The PSAs on this unit were the trailblazers for the rest of the hospital and were a resource to other units beginning implementation of the new role.

As the PSA role evolved, it was imperative to have consistency in competencies among the departments. A competency-based orientation tool was developed, which focused on performance criteria, learning options, and an evaluation mechanism. Also, a unit-based Patient Services Assistant Quality Control Assurance Program was established. This ensured that units were maintaining proper care and housekeeping standards. A QA check-sheet was developed, which is completed by the Environmental Services Department as part of its quarterly surveys of the units.

Postimplementation Problems Implementation of the program has not been without problems. It was hoped that all housekeepers and unit makers would be interested in applying for the new role. But a number chose not to apply, which necessitated hiring from outside the organization. Personnel hired from outside without housekeeping experience required a more extensive orientation. Recruiting and retaining people in these positions have continued to be challenges. Adding to the problem was a misinterpretation of the job description by individuals applying for a PSA position. The recruitment ad implied more focus on patient care than on housekeeping and indirect care. The ad was revised but even after the revision, recruiting problems still exist for some of the patient care areas. It appears that the medical/surgical areas have had the best success in retaining individuals, with less success in the more technical areas.

However, in most patient care areas, the PSA role is working well, especially when the opportunity exists for patient contact. In these areas, there truly is a team effort and strong support for keeping the program in place. On the other hand, in areas where the job is mainly housekeeping duties with little patient contact, PSA turnover is more frequent. This has been a difficult issue to understand, but there is a sense that there may be less job satisfaction due to less patient contact, or it could be that expectations do not match the job in those areas. It is possible that some patient care areas may benefit by going back to using the centralized housekeeping department. We are in the process of evaluating the role on certain patient care units and deciding if we might need to resume the housekeeping role in some areas while using the PSA role in others.

Responses to Patient Care Needs

It has become apparent that patient care needs are driving roles to be redefined and restructured. The following subsections describe two examples at Gundersen Lutheran: expanding the LPN role and decentralizing the infusion therapy role.

Expanding the Licensed Practical Nurse Role

With the PSA program up and running and supporting the professional nurse in indirect aspects of care, nursing leadership began to look at creating a multiskilled technician role. The number of available LPN programs was declining, and it was clear that our future supply of LPNs would be problematic. We felt it was necessary to develop a role that would be similar but require less education. The purpose of this new role was to reduce the number of staff members whom patients were exposed to in the course of their stay. The role would incorporate responsibilities in phlebotomy, simple respiratory function, and physical therapy, occupational therapy support, and current nursing assistant and technician responsibilities. We decided to call the position patient care technician. Initially, we considered filling the role with nursing assistants and technicians trained in the new skills we developed. We worked with the local technical college to determine how to use currently offered courses to provide additional knowledge, expertise, and skills necessary for the new role.

However, as we drew closer to finalizing the job description, training, and competencies, the collective bargaining unit challenged the new patient care technician role and obtained a ruling to include it as part of the bargaining unit. The nursing assistants were part of the collective bargaining unit, but our technicians, phlebotomists, respiratory technicians, and physical and occupational assistants were not. Incorporating some of their responsibilities into this role might open these positions up to becoming part of the collective bargaining unit as well. Faced with this possibility, we reevaluated the role to determine if we wanted to move ahead with it as defined. After much discussion, we decided not to pursue development of the patient care technician role. Instead, we looked at our current number of LPNs and realized we could expand on their current job responsibilities by incorporating some of the newly identified skills into their role. The LPN role was actually a better route as this group of individuals already had the education and expertise required for the new role. They could be trained in any skills essential to their new responsibilities. Because the LPN role has never been part of the collective bargaining unit, we were able to use this role for some of the requirements of the proposed technician role. Again, our challenge was to avoid taking away responsibilities that were part of the collective bargaining unit's responsibilities.

Thus, we were forced to evaluate the skill mix of the patient care units that would be using the newly expanded role of the LPN. Again, we needed to look at having the right person doing the right job. This process helped us identify where LPNs were most needed versus nursing assistants and technicians. The goal was to reduce the number of skill mixes and the number of contacts a patient encountered on patient care units. This resulted in shifting some LPNs and nursing assistants among units.

In 1995, we looked at decentralizing phlebotomy on the units with high phlebotomy needs. With the help of our technical college and hospital lab department, the LPNs were trained in phlebotomy, which has now been incorporated into their role. This has resulted in their ability to maintain direct care accountability to patients while being able to individualize procedures based on patient needs. A benefit to patients is that LPNs can respond to their needs when they are drawing blood. This was not the case with the phlebotomy technicians, who were not trained to assist patients with many of their requests. Because phlebotomy was a centralized function before becoming decentralized to the unit-based LPNs, this change has improved the efficiency of patient care. Currently, we continue to have sufficient LPNs to provide the necessary coverage, but we may be faced with reevaluating the role in the future if LPN numbers decline.

Decentralizing the Infusion Therapy Role

The IV therapy role existed at Gundersen Lutheran for more than 25 years. Infusion care was limited to the acute care setting and was rarely found in the ambulatory and home care settings. Up until the past 10 years, only 10 to 15 percent of all Gundersen's acute care patients had a peripheral IV in place. In 1980, the average census at Gundersen Lutheran Hospital was 350 patients per day; therefore, approximately 35 to 40 patients received IV therapy daily. This number was not enough to keep the RNs on the patient care units proficient in performing IV therapy. With this in mind, specialists for peripheral IV starts and maintenance became an IV team for the hospital. Improved expertise and implementation of infusion therapy standards resulted in fewer unsuccessful attempts to insert the IV, fewer infections, and increased patient satisfaction.

Today, the environment has changed and the number of patients receiving infusion therapy at Gundersen Lutheran is 95 percent of the average daily census, which is 170 patients in the acute care setting and 100 patients in the same-day medicine, same-day surgery, and ambulatory care settings. The number of infusion therapy patients has increased from 40 per day to 256 per day. In addition, central lines and peripherally inserted central catheters (PICC) are inserted in a large number of patients in all settings. With the great increase of infusion therapy for patients, there are plenty of opportunities to insert and care for peripheral IVs on most patient care units. This led us to look at decentralizing infusion therapy.

In March 1996, we began to explore the role of the IV therapist. Using the guiding principles of the 1988 redesign efforts for professional nursing, the IV Department began to analyze and design a new role for infusion therapy. The department, along with unit RN representatives, designed the following plan to decentralize infusion therapy to meet the patient care needs of the twenty-first century:

- The responsibilities of basic IV assessment and care were incorporated into the case associate role. (This included discontinuing and capping IVs, ongoing assessment of IV sites, documentation, and dressing care of peripheral sites.)
- A small group of care providers (RNs or LPNs) on each unit was educated and trained to become the unit-based IV therapy team and started routine peripheral IVs. (This improved the timeliness for IV starts and initiation of IV medications by nurses who had developed a relationship with the patient.)
- The unit-based IV staff developed a team relationship with all health care professionals to incorporate infusion therapy as part of the overall plan of care.
- The responsibilities of the original hospital IV team were expanded to form a Core Infusion Therapy Department

that spans the patient care continuum (inpatient, outpatient, and home care). Their responsibilities are to

—back up and troubleshoot complex infusion therapy needs;

—insert PICC catheters for acute, ambulatory, and home care patients;

—ensure that infusion therapy care plans for patients are implemented and followed across the continuum;

—disseminate education related to infusion therapy to patients, families, and all health care providers throughout the continuum; and

—assist with maintaining the core competencies, practice guidelines, policies, procedures, and state-of-the-art technology for infusion therapy.

• The Core Infusion Therapy Department assists with annual proficiency verification of all staff performing infusion therapy in all settings.

In most health care institutions, all RNs are expected to perform infusion therapy. To maintain the quality control of a centralized IV therapy department and yet move to a patient-driven care model, a core group of unit-based RNs will perform basic infusion therapy for patients on their units. The new Core Infusion Therapy Department will provide the backup to those units, perform complex infusion therapy, and be responsible for maintenance of the competencies of all staff performing infusion therapy.

Conclusion

Across the country, patient-centered care has taken root. However, the care delivery at Gundersen Lutheran is more than patient centered; it is an example of synergistic patient care. Curley describes what we are actualizing at Gundersen Lutheran in the following excerpt: "Patients' characteristics drive nurses' competencies. When patients' characteristics and nurses' competencies match and synergize, patients' outcomes may be optimized." The premise of the synergy model, "is to recognize the combined actions of both the patient and the nurse."[9]

The patient care delivery model at Gundersen Lutheran is dynamic. The vice president for nursing's creativity and vision for patient-centered care have been a driving force and kept the patient at the heart of our changes. The guiding principles kept us moving forward and on target, even when faced with obstacles. At times, it seemed we were at a standstill, but when we looked at what our goals were, we were able to be creative and accomplish what we set out to do. According to Noer, there are four levels of intervention in restructuring: process, grieving, empowerment, and systems.[10] These can be applied either by an outside consultant or internally, if the organization has a leader who is skilled at facilitation and interpersonal relationships. We, as a nursing department under inspirational leadership, were empowered to design our care delivery, using the resources we had available in a way that would meet our needs. This is not always the case in organizations where consultants are used to drive changes.

Recently, Gundersen Lutheran was recognized as one of the best 100 hospitals in the country. We have consistently demonstrated short lengths of stay and high patient satisfaction. Our redesign efforts have played a major part in this. We will continue to look at how to be the best of the best!

References

1. M. Wheatley, *Leadership and the New Science* (San Francisco, CA: Barrett-Koehler Publishers, 1993), p. 13.

2. B. Johnson, S. Friend, and J. MacDonald, "Nurses' Changing and Emerging Roles with Use of Unlicensed Assistive Personnel," in *Nursing Roles Evolving or Recycled?* S. Moorehead, ed. (Thousand Oaks, CA: Sage Publications, 1997), p. 81.

3. M. L. Gerke and M. K. Proksch, "Socialization into the Differentiated Nursing Roles of Case Manager and Case Associate," thesis, Department of Nursing, Winona State University, Winona, MN, 1995, p 30.

4. J. Larson, "The Healing We: A Transformative Model for Nursing," *Nursing & Health Care* 13, no. 5 (1992): 248.

5. J. Koerner and K. L. Karpiuk, *Implementing Differentiated Practice: Transformation by Design* (Gaithersburg, MD: Aspen Publishers, 1994), p. 39.

6. J. B. Doerge and N. R. Hagenow, "Integrating Care Delivery," *Nursing Admininistration Quarterly* 20, no. 2 (1996): 42–48.

7. L. Strasen, "Redesigning Hospitals around Patients and Technology," *Nursing Economic$* 9, no. 4 (1991): 234.

8. J. B. Doerge and N. R. Hagenow, "Integrating Care Delivery," *Nursing Administration Quarterly* 20, no. 2 (1996): 42–48.

9. M. A. Q. Curley, "Patient-Nurse Synergy: Optimizing Patients' Outcomes," *American Journal of Critical Care* 7, no. 1 (1998): 64.

10. D. Noer, "Solutions for Surviving Restructuring," *[Hansen & Washburn's] Successful Restructuring* 1, no. 1 (June 1996): 8.

CHAPTER FOUR

Adopting the Integrated
Team Management Model

Bonnie Michaels, RN, MA
Mary K. Stull, RN, PhD

Elmhurst Memorial Hospital is a full-service, not-for-profit community hospital in Elmhurst, Illinois, that has 400-plus beds, treats 40,000 patients annually, and has 96,000 outpatient visits. It is one component of the Elmhurst Memorial System, which includes home health and hospice care, a management systems organization, a physician-hospital organization, and primary care clinics at three suburban sites.

This case study looks at the decision by Elmhurst Memorial Hospital to restructure its patient care services division using an integrated team management model that focuses on team management.

Impetus for Change

Executive teams, multidisciplinary teams, interdisciplinary teams, quality improvement teams, self-managed teams—in a recent survey of the business and health care literature, the word *team* appeared in over 4,000 entries. Is the establishment and utilization of teams a health care fad? According to Ulschak and SnowAntle, health care can no longer function effectively without teams.[1] The increasing volatility of the health care industry has resulted in information too complex for an individual to interpret in isolation. Combined with shorter lead times to prepare for change, this rapid flow of information necessitates a think-tank approach to planning, ideally involving diverse ideas and people.

Although these arguments for teams are compelling, we all have experienced disappointments in team performance. Curtain aptly points out that people are often forced into teams.[2] Although many of us love our work, we may not have the skills or desire to function well in a team. Hart highlights these issues: "The best and brightest are brought together in hopes that their individual talents will add up to something more than the sum of the parts. 'Synergy,' we say, rubbing our hands in anticipation. Too often, however, mediocre results mock our great expectations. The pattern is numbingly familiar."[3]

At Elmhurst Memorial Hospital, Patient Care Services was torn between two seemingly conflicting positions: the belief that a strong strategic-thinking leadership team was needed to lead the department into the new millennium and the experience that many team efforts provide disappointing results. In view of rapidly emerging demands to provide high-quality, cost-effective care across the continuum, disappointing results were not an acceptable alternative. With all this in mind, we decided to carefully select a group of health care professionals who would assume full accountability for all quality and cost outcomes in their service areas and, equally important, function as a seamless interdependent team to meet those ends.

The hospital organization was structured along a traditional medical model design, with various departments reporting to their respective vice presidents (ancillary services, nursing services, human resources, financial services, and so on). The organization was financially strong and, until four years ago, was not in the position of having to address the cost of providing care. However, the pressure from managed care to provide high-quality service at low cost began to mount. In addition, hospital networks were forming in the Chicago area, and with contracting for health care services overriding personal choice for health care providers, physicians, and health care organizations, Elmhurst was beginning to feel the heat from the competition.

Foundation for a New Organizational Design

The new team was created through a conceptual framework first described by Griffith. In his work on health care redesign, he contended that changes in organizations occur best through clinical teams influencing clinical processes formerly controlled solely by individual practitioners. He emphasized that teams can cut across traditional accountability hierarchies and accept accountability with less supervision. Thus, as care moves from the inpatient to the outpatient venue, the direct supervision of caregivers decreases.[4]

Elmhurst Memorial's board of trustees and executive management made the improvement of relationships with the hospital's physician groups a high priority. This identified goal was to be accomplished by the integration of patient care services following specific guidelines for care with the foundation of continuous improvement processes. Although known to be extremely conservative, the board supported the needed restructuring.

The goal was easy to talk about but difficult to achieve. A change in organizational philosophy was needed. Clinicians needed to become cost effective in the provision of care, and integration of cross-disciplinary teams became more crucial. "Health care must become more integrated through permanent teams oriented around specific clinical conditions, led by specialists most familiar with that condition."[5]

The Case for Teams in Health Care

"Health care is a team sport."[6] Because of their personal professional identity, licensure, education, and expertise, over time many health care professionals build a multitude of fiefdoms or silos that fragment into professional, departmental kingdoms, each with its own language and customs. Only those authorized may enter; those who intrude are made to feel they are outsiders. Ulschak and SnowAntle described this phenomenon but also emphasized the need for these groups to work interdependently.

> Various highly trained professionals depend on one another to get the work of the health care organization done. In order for the deserved outcome to be reached, the whole health care team has to work together. We are talking about systems thinking here. Systems define the components of health care organizations and the relationship between these components. In order for the system to work effectively, all those components and relationships need to be synchronized.[7]

The goal of synchronized interdependence of the Elmhurst Memorial Hospital team took over three years to achieve. A team is "two or more persons who are engaged in a common goal who are dependent on one another for results and who have joint accountability for results."[8] The organization that can effectively manage interdependence has a distinct competitive advantage. The integration of services creates satisfactory experiences for patients and their families, physicians and patients, and hospital employees and customers, greatly enhancing hospital marketability. Strategic challenges and team achievements strengthen the team. Members continually learn from each other. They also model the behaviors for others within the organization. As goals are achieved and accomplishments are recognized, the team gains more motivation and strength to tackle new problems for the future.

MacGregor identified the following criteria of an effective team:

1. The team understands its primary task and its primary reason for being.
2. Open communication, telling the truth, and giving feedback are valued.
3. Mutual trust is earned.

4. Mutual support is given and individual members support each other.
5. Recognizing individual differences and managing the diversity and uniqueness of each member can only make a team more effective.
6. The team is used selectively when it is needed for a specific purpose and more than one person is needed to get the job done.
7. The members of the team are skilled in feedback, management of conflict, and group process.
8. Each member of the team is an effective leader who can define issues, mission, and goals and identify how the vision, mission, and goals can be met.[9]

The patient care programs in Elmhurst Memorial System's framework for the delivery of care have forged a closer affiliation with the medical staff, opened the decision-making process to those with the strongest clinical expertise, and enhanced professional dialogue and strengthened infrastructure for good decision-making processes. The relationship and organization of the components of the system are founded on the principles of patient-focused care and decision making as a dynamic process requiring broad participation in a multidisciplinary, continuous improvement process. Its goals are to continuously improve quality, reduce costs, and manage growth. Figure 4-1 shows the conceptual relationships between the medical model and the integrated team management model.

An Integrated Team Management Model

Dedicated to providing the highest-quality care across the continuum, patient care services adopted a program line team management model in which all ancillary services support the product lines reporting to the vice president of patient care services. Figure 4-2 shows the components of the program line team management model.

Figure 4-1. Elmhurst Memorial Hospital Organizational Chart

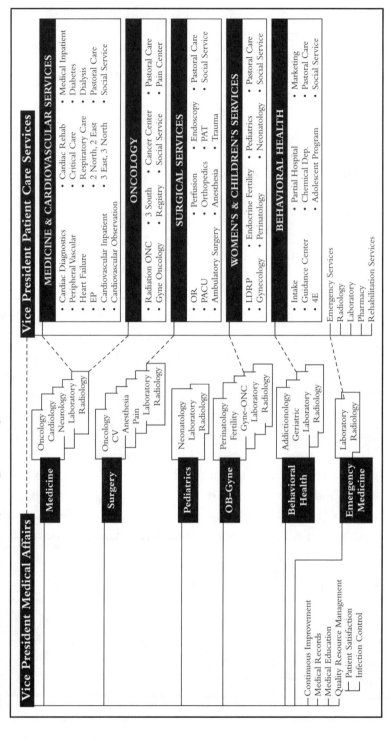

Figure 4-2. Patient Care Services Team

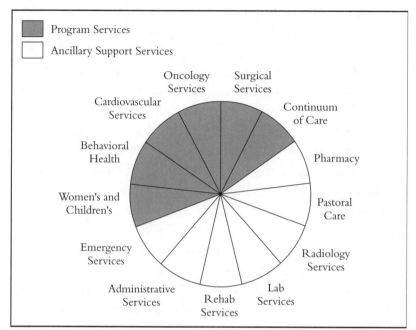

As the figure shows, patient care services encompass the following programs:

- *Cardiovascular services:* This program is led by a program director and three program managers. Program responsibilities encompass inpatient and outpatient services, including an inpatient telemetry unit; a 26-bed intensive care unit that services medical, surgical, and cardiac patients (all nurses are cross-trained); a heart failure center; and a cardiac rehabilitative program. Also within the program are cardiac diagnostic services, which include EKG and cath labs; respiratory therapy; a sleep disorder program; a comprehensive interdisciplinary diabetes education center; a 36-bed medical multispecialty unit; and a renal dialysis unit that treats 90 patients each week.
- *Surgical services:* This program addresses all perioperative programming including preadmission testing, ambulatory

surgery, 13-room OR suite, PACU, open heart program, orthopedic/surgical inpatient unit, a 5-room endoscopy suite, anesthesia services, and the sterile processing department. This program is managed by a director of surgical services, two program managers, and a specialty coordinator.

- *Oncology services:* This program is managed by a program director and one program manager. It integrates inpatient and outpatient services that include a 38-bed inpatient oncology unit, an outpatient cancer center, radiation oncology services, an outpatient chronic center for pain management, and a tumor registry.

- *Behavioral health services:* This program is directed by a program director, one manager, and several clinical coordinators. It includes an inpatient psychiatric unit; mental health clinic; child, adolescent, adult, and older adult programs; and dual diagnosis programming. In addition, the services include a partial hospital program, a 24-hour crisis program and intake center, and EAP services that are offered to the community, including local business and industry. These programs are offered in multiple sites across the continuum. The program is different from the others in that it has a community advisory board and its own marketing, quality assurance, and utilization review staff.

- *Women's and children's services:* This program is directed by a program manager and three clinical coordinators who provide support and direction for a 26-bed, integrated labor, delivery, recovery, and postpartum unit; a neonatal care unit; infertility services; a pediatric program for inpatients; pediatric ambulatory surgery; and a pediatric preadmission testing service.

- *Continuum of Care program:* This program is directed by an executive director, two managers, and a coordinator of social services. It encompasses a wholly owned subsidiary of hospital-based home health services that covers a 30-mile service area. It has its own board of trustees and community advisory committee. The Continuum of Care program also includes a 38-bed skilled nursing facility and a hospice that sees 200 patients a year. The director also provides leadership to the system for discharge planning/social work services.

In addition to the above programs, other clinical ancillary support departments were realigned under the direction of the vice president of patient care services because their function was the provision of patient care. These departments included emergency services, pastoral services, laboratory and pathology services, pharmacy services, radiology services, rehabilitation services, and administrative support services (including a financial analyst and nurse staffing support services).

Flattening of the Management Structure

The clinical and ancillary services that make up the patient care services division originally were administratively directed by two vice presidents. When the delivery of care model was redesigned, the vice president of ancillary services position was eliminated, creating an organizational structure that supported an integrated approach to health care delivery through one person who acts as leader, coach, and mentor directing an integrated team. The single leader has a vision of the team, defines the vision, gains team buy-in, and develops a collaborative team process based on consensus. The result is a shared vision. The following goals comprise the vision underlying the reorganization:

- Aggressively attend to patients' demands for service
- Streamline accountability
- Set directions for the future
- Provide program excellence while controlling cost and enhancing quality

In addition, the reorganization eliminated layers of management in nursing services: supervisors, nurse managers, and assistant nurse managers. Ancillary services eliminated multiple directors, managers, and coordinators as well, redefined and merged sections, and became a flatter, more functional organization.

The roles of department heads were evaluated. The position of director was redefined, becoming accountable for large, complex programs like the cardiovascular program. The program manager role was created to be accountable for the management of either smaller, less complex service lines or to run sections of larger, more complex programs. Span of control was increased so that program managers managed 70 to 100 full-time-equivalent employees (FTEs). Both the directors and the program managers are department heads. With fewer managerial positions, a core value was realized as staff were encouraged to solve problems at the point of service.

The change resulted in the elimination of bureaucracy by giving staff in each program the ability to meet their own customers' needs. We hoped to create newly developed processes that were innovative in thought and practice. There have been promising signs that staff are fully engaged in this new approach to problem solving. For example, very recently the Family Birthing Center was experiencing an extremely high census. As a result, seven mothers who were to be discharged in the evening needed to be offered an earlier discharge in order to accommodate the LDRP space for active laboring patients. To make this option more attractive, staff offered the new mothers dinner vouchers and theatre tickets if they would select the early discharge option. Three of the seven mothers enthusiastically accepted. The physicians involved supported the staff's solution and the three patients were discharged within the hour. This ability to solve problems, take the initiative, and appropriately follow through is a sure sign that staff can prioritize patient care needs and generate alternatives to meet patient care and institutional needs.

Of key importance was understanding the patient population, customer needs, and the core strengths of each program along with the ability to respond to changing environmental factors. Under the direction of one leader, a shared vision brought the team together. The team members identified what they had in common and used each individual's strengths to make the team strong and effective.

The flattening of the organizational structure depended on the size of each programmatic need. What was important was the individual's competence in interpersonal communication, problem solving, and the ability to articulate and advocate a personal vision. This endeavor required team members to get to know each other through constant communication, active dialogue, and constant clarification for evolving their thinking and approach to problem solving. "If members of an organization do not spend sufficient time discussing and evolving their own mental models in interactions with their leaders, conflicting and competing visions begin developing within the organization.[10]

Redefinition of Leadership Responsibilities

As the vice president developed the new service lines, the role of the leader of each service line program was further defined. Complexity of the program, number of services offered, FTE budget, and total expense budgets were all reviewed before appointments to the respective roles were made. The titles of program director (for large complex programs) and program manager (for smaller programs) were used to differentiate span of control and accountability. Both program directors and program managers were responsible for patient service, customer satisfaction, growth initiatives, community marketing and education, professional collaboration, and positive clinical outcomes. (Two programs have established community advisory boards. The presence of an advisory board, composed of many different representatives of the community, is crucial not only to receiving real-time information on existing needs and feedback about current programming but also is an effective way to market services to those who need them.) All program leaders have developed interdisciplinary strategic growth plans with the active participation of the patient care services' team and a diverse group of physicians who are using the program's services. It is here that the vision and skills of the patient care services leadership team are necessary and often tested.

Use of Group Process in Decision Making

The original team members did not know each other well. Nursing managers traditionally had kept issues among themselves and had a level of comfort with each other as an identified professional group with the same educational background. The support services leaders, too, had been more comfortable working as individually defined groups and departments with a commonality of purpose, and seeking out others for problem solving was rare. Group process in problem solving was new and felt strange—easy for some members to adjust to and hard for others. Team members often discussed common normative and non-normative behaviors and how to gain trust and mutual respect for each other. Slowly, they started to seek out each other for problem resolution. Mini subteams were created with a charge to solve problems together. These activities were often challenging. While arriving at solutions, team members learned to share issues and develop mutual respect for each other.

Team-Think Innovations and Initiatives

The group's increasing comfort led to more integrated risk taking, and innovative projects were realized. As a result, new services within the programs were soon developed. For example, a new patient service—the home IV infusion program—was identified as a growth initiative. The directors of home health and pharmacy planned and developed the proposal together. To avoid costly start-up, the director of laboratory services, who also managed a large reference lab business, offered his van delivery courier service to provide the transport support that was needed.

Another illustration of "team think" in the process of leadership development was our approach to how we could financially support community needs for preventive health. A parish nurse program was developed by the coordinator of pastoral care and the director of home health and supported by the home health program and a local community church that offered congregational support and space. Combining goals of supplying the needed services to community churches through inventive thought has resulted in a very successful program that has gained community support.

A third example of innovation was the acquisition of a large physician group practice clinic (32 physicians), lab services, radiology services, and pharmacy services. With the shift from physician-run management to hospital management, these redefined off-site services are managed more effectively by team members. Clear, consistent standards have resulted in higher patient and physician satisfaction with less service cost to the community.

Finally, another initiative addressed the issue of which services and processes to centralize or decentralize. In the past, poor planning had resulted in frequent transfers of patients from one location or treatment area to another. For example, rehabilitation services centralized on the first floor extended patient wait times, causing backup and adding patient transport time to and from therapies. Continuous improvement teams, consisting predominantly of patient care services managers, staff, and physicians, addressed appropriate allocation of specific services for each program. Teams that achieved their goals were the Patient Care Services Management Team, Heart Pain Evaluation Team, Heart Failure Team, Observation Status Team, Centralized Transportation Team, Discharge Planning Team, Preadmission Testing Team, and Admission/Transfer/ Discharge Team. These teams reviewed the locations of ancillary services to better identify process, efficiency, and clinical support for each patient population. As a result, the following initiatives were accomplished:

- Program and unit-based rehabilitation services were created.
- The Cardiac Rehabilitation Center and the Diabetes Center were relocated in the cardiovascular service line.
- The opening of a heart pain evaluation/observation unit in the cardiovascular program was implemented in record time with full Emergency Department and Cardiology Department physician support.
- The Heart Failure Center was relocated and expanded.
- The Heart Center was established with all comprehensive services on the same floor.
- A medical 23-hour observation unit with its own dedicated staff was opened.
- A central transportation program to relieve nursing staff from transport activity was implemented.
- The Ambulatory Surgery Center's preadmission testing functions were decentralized to Surgical Services, Cardiovascular Services, and Pediatric Services to best meet programmatic needs, nursing skills, and expertise to enhance patient care services programmatically.
- Home health liaison nurses were offered an integral role in discharge planning.
- Dedicated pharmacists, rehabilitation staff, social workers, chaplains, and dietitians were assigned to each program team.
- Pharmacists began conducting patient rounds with nurses and became available to physicians as consultants.

Long Road to Trust

When the patient care services team was newly formed, members identified the need to learn more about each other. The team leader, the vice president of patient care services, initiated team development. Together with the vice president, the team needed to challenge any perceptions that individuals might have developed over time. The group decided that it needed to spend time away from the day-to-day pressures of managing its own clinical operations and move to a new milieu to learn how to work together. A facilitator was selected and the team headed to George Williams College near Lake Geneva, Wisconsin, a wooded retreat for an outward-bound experience that would be mentally and physically challenging. The team leader chose to be a full member of the group, leaving it up to the facilitator to challenge the group to approach problem solving in new, inventive ways. Individuals completed initial written assessments on how they rated the team's progress in working together, its problem-solving and leadership skills, and what they wanted to achieve during the two-day retreat. This program was so successful that it has become a group ritual each year.

In addition, we videotaped the activities we used in group process problem solving and were able to watch and analyze our group dynamics. We also used another assessment tool, the Kiersey Temperament Sorter, which sorts personality and temperament preferences of individuals.[11] As the team reviewed, evaluated, and openly discussed the individual and group results, we gained an understanding of our own management style. We began to appreciate the differences in our approaches to problem solving. We were then able to understand and adapt to differences in individual management styles. As a result, we learned to communicate more effectively as a team.

The retreats invariably bring in new members. How they are welcomed, worked with, and accepted are crucial to the team's success. At the most recent retreat, a new member said she felt it was an honor and a challenge to be part of the team and hoped she could meet the expectations of the group. This message was both a compliment and a concern. A discussion ensued on how the group was perceived as being intimidating to this new member. This perception surprised the long-standing members; they felt it needed to be discussed. The new member needed the assurance of acceptance and support.

In these annual retreats we role play and act out ritualistic roles and positions we all assume when trying to resolve real problems within the organization. In a nonstressful, energizing environment, we are able to identify our weaknesses and the old roles we fall back into. The process allows us to explore all sides of an issue and to appreciate the benefits of more than one course of action. As a result, the team creates more successful patterns of behavior and discards the old unsuccessful ones. Team members learn how to conquer their fears by working together to achieve a particularly difficult goal. We have all tested ourselves through challenging courses. Many of us realize that we can accomplish and achieve so much more if we work together. We hold each other accountable. We have gained a new understanding of the strong bond we have developed and the nature of the contributions we each make for the team to be successful. We have learned not only our own roles in the team, but the contextual relationships we have formed in the group.

The dynamics of the group have changed over time. An instinct has developed among the members as to when they need to collaborate. Often a member doesn't need to be asked, but offers to assist another who is struggling to solve a particular issue. The results of an ongoing team dynamics and team effectiveness survey over three years illustrate how integrated a group the team has become.

Outcomes

The patient care services team has experienced many successes across the boundaries of cost and quality. Many service areas and programs have grown, with a corresponding drop in expenses and a growth in patient satisfaction. Dynamics within the group are strong and members are committed to continued growth.

Since 1994, our direct cost per case has dropped 20 percent for both inpatients and outpatients. We attribute these savings in part to the ability of our team to solve problems across service lines. In addition, our ability to support one another and our staffs during the difficult periods of staff reductions and major change initiatives have allowed us to emerge as a stronger team.

The strength of our team is readily apparent when examining the changes in our perceptions of group commitment and performance. Prior to our off-site retreats, each team member responded to questions regarding interdependence of the team, open communication, and trust among members. Table 4-1 highlights the dramatic change in our scores from 1995 to 1997.

A more important outcome is our ability to maintain and improve our overall patient satisfaction scores. Presently, the satisfaction with nursing and ancillary care is at an overall high of 8.96 out of a 10-point scale. Implementation of CI team recommendations, rapid resolution of patient complaints, and high visibility of our management staff have resulted in these findings.

Conclusion

The Patient Care Services Team at Elmhurst Memorial Hospital is a matrix of diverse disciplines that has come together as an operating structure that stresses integration, lateral coordination, and sharing of efforts. The team openly supports an aggressive, enthusiastic approach to daily problem solving. Through team cooperation and collaboration, the members' professional respect for each other is continually growing. They take pride in the team's achievements, and their enthusiasm is perpetually fed by interaction. Dwyer believes that the quality of our lives is very much a function of our ability to influence people in myriad relationships.[12]

Relationship building provides people with an incentive to influence others. There is no limit to an individual's potential for influencing others. Accepting the risks and understanding human motivation to change behavior is all it takes.

Table 4-1. Team Effectiveness Scores (10-Point Scale)

	1995	1997
Interdependence	3.13	7.08
Open communication	4.00	7.41
Trust	3.75	7.45

In health care organizations the rapid rate of change, the ability to adjust and respond, the challenge to address complex problems, and the imperative to succeed all require the investment of time to create strong teams. New values and norms and a shared awareness of the need to strengthen working alliances through teamwork is the foundation of effective teams. Only through this process will creative, innovative solutions emerge.

References

1. F. L. Ulschak and S. M. SnowAntle, *Team Architecture: The Manager's Guide to Designing Effective Work Teams* (Ann Arbor, MI: Health Administration Press, 1995).

2. L. Curtain, "Jonathan Livingston Seagull on Teams," *Nursing Management* (Springhouse, PA: Springhouse Corporation, 1998), pp. 5–6.

3. E. Hart, "Leadership Teams," *Executive Excellence* (July 1996): 9–10.

4. J. R. Griffith, V. K. Sahney, and R. A. Mohr, *Reengineering Health Care: Building on CQI* (Ann Arbor, MI: Health Administration Press, 1995) p. 128.

5. Ibid., p.132.

6. F. L. Ulschak and S. M. SnowAntle, *Team Architecture: The Manager's Guide to Designing Effective Work Teams* (Ann Arbor, MI: Health Administration Press, 1995), p. 1.

7. Ibid., p. 5.

8. Ibid., p. 8.

9. W. B. Reddy, *Team Building* (San Diego: University Associates, 1988), p. 10.

10. J. R. Griffith, V. K. Sahney, and R. A. Mohr, *Reengineering Health Care: Building on CQI* (Ann Arbor, MI: Health Administration Press, 1995), p. 29.

11. D. Kiersey and M. Bates, *The Sixteen Types from Please Understand Me* (Del Mar, CA: Prometheus Nemesis Book Co., 1996).

12. S. Roven and L. Ginsberg, *Managing Hospitals: Lessons from the Johnson & Johnson Wharton Fellows Program for Nurses* (San Francisco: Jossey-Bass Publishers, 1991), p. 177.

CHAPTER FIVE

Reengineering the Patient Care Delivery System through Care Management

Norma J. Ferdinand, DNSc, MSN, RN

Lancaster General Hospital (LGH) is a 500-bed community hospital in southeastern Pennsylvania. It is one of the five busiest hospitals in the state, and comparative statistics (both state and national) consistently demonstrate that the care provided ranks among the best. An acute care facility within the integrated delivery system of Lancaster Health Alliance (LHA), LGH made the Mercer/HCIA list of "100 Top Hospitals: Benchmarks for Success" for the past two years.[1] The list's purpose is to identify the U.S. hospitals delivering the most cost-efficient and highest-quality medical care based on financial, clinical, and operational measures. To be on the list, a hospital must have a thorough understanding of its strengths and weaknesses and demonstrate a willingness to make changes that will integrate best practices into all phases of its operations.[2]

This case study describes the development, implementation, and expansion of a care management program at Lancaster

General Hospital from 1995 to the present. The model includes both an inpatient case management program and a community-based program.

Impetus for Change

LHA's mission is to provide a system for delivering a spectrum of superior services that meets the health care needs of the people of Lancaster and the surrounding region through continuous quality improvement. It is this philosophy of health care delivery and community service that supports the continued development and refinement of systems and processes to provide not only the best-quality care, but also the best value for the community. Figure 5-1 shows a few of the programs LHA has implemented.

Pennsylvania has a very high proportion of the elderly, second only to Florida in the proportion of residents 65 years old or older. The senior population in Lancaster County is increasing, and the frail elderly population (> age 75 with comorbid conditions) is expected to grow by 24 percent between 1990 and 2000.[3] LGH recognized that problems with the traditional patient care delivery systems (particularly for the chronically ill and elderly) included the following:

- Fragmentation of care and services
- Difficulty accessing the array of available services due to a patient's lack of knowledge about resources and how to use them
- Emphasis on care that is episodic and illness oriented
- Preventable readmissions and adverse outcomes as a result of unmonitored hospital discharges of high-risk individuals
- Increased health care costs often resulting from patients receiving care and services in an acute care setting instead of less expensive community care alternatives
- Absence of a systematic approach to patient care delivery

Figure 5-1. Programs Implemented at Lancaster General Hospital

- Patient-focused care
- Community wellness programs
- Level II Trauma Program
- Five-Star Caring Initiative
- Innovative employee orientation program
- Seniors Program and Geriatric Assessment Team
- Integrated IS and decision support systems
- Care Management Program
  —Acute care
  —Community-based

Factors in the health care market that precipitated a need for change include the following:

- Health care financing and reimbursement changes
- Increasing client expectations and demands for access and control of health care
- Increased health care costs
- Emphasis on lifetime health care management
- Provider reorganizations with improved physician and hospital relationships

Introduction of the Care Management Model

The first step in 1994 in creating the care management model at LGH was to understand the organization's strengths and weaknesses. The following strengths were identified:

- A reputation for being a high-quality, low-cost care provider
- An established Community Wellness Program (including a Center for Wellness and a Seniors Program)
- A successful inpatient case management process for a select subpopulation of patients (cardiac surgery)

- Decision support and outcome management capabilities for measuring cost and clinical outcomes in the inpatient setting
- A network for lifetime care available within the LHA (acute care, home care, hospice, infusion therapy and medical equipment, rehabilitation, transitional and long-term care, outpatient services, preventive care, and so on)
- Primary care focus within the Lancaster General Medical Group (a network of primary care and specialty care medical practices organized in 1995 by LHA)
- Commitment of $25 million over five years for an integrated information services system

Among the organization's weaknesses were the following:

- Lack of a process for using available data and modifying medical and nursing practice based on patient care outcomes
- Fragmentation of care and services between acute care settings and community and primary care providers
- Emphasis on the acute care environment
- Decentralized approach to development of critical paths with no established standards or comprehensive outcome measurement process

The framework of the LGH care management model was established based on the following assumptions:

- Variations in patient care processes produce variations in outcomes. Standardizing key patient care processes and using a systematic team approach for evaluation and modification would achieve improved outcomes.
- Organizing and managing services around the functions of patient care and the entire care continuum would have a favorable impact on patient care outcomes.
- Reorganizing the patient care delivery system was necessary to better accommodate the health care needs of the community members on a lifetime continuum of care.

- A continued emphasis on health promotion was necessary to reduce the future cost structure for health care.

Building a Foundation for a Population-Based Managed Care Approach

The visionary for the care management model was the senior vice president of patient care services for LHA. She organized and led a project design task force with representation from all disciplines believed to be affected by, or involved with, promoting a change in patient care delivery. The task force consisted of staff from different departments, skill levels, and seniority. Its responsibility was to design a care management system that responded to the needs of the patient across the continuum with increasing emphasis on the effectiveness and efficiency of the patient care process. The decisions and components the task force was responsible for included the following:

- Conceptual and theoretical framework for care management
- Description of services provided and predicted outcomes
- Proposal for centralized department of care management versus a decentralized program
- Targeted patient populations, predicted volumes, and expected outcomes
- Staffing requirements and job descriptions
- Resource requirements
- Financial feasibility analysis and proposed budget
- Education and communication plan
- Management structure
- Timeline for proposal development and implementation

In this phase, a distinction was made between care management and case management as follows:

- *Care management* is viewed as a population-based approach to care delivery that supports high-quality patient care and ensures appropriate and cost-effective use of resources for a patient population. The objective is to ensure that the care provided in different settings at different times and by different professionals supports common patient and system goals. Care management focuses on the needs of a patient population and uses tools such as critical paths, medical management guidelines, protocols, and standardized physician orders to provide consistent best practice of care. One of its strengths is that it can be used by all members of the health care team and by all competency levels of nursing personnel (from novice to expert). The plan of care remains consistent even though individual caregivers change. Care management encompasses the needs of like individuals—over time and over multiple episodes of care—and helps to establish the best practices of care in order to meet those needs. All patients need their *care managed;* however, not every patient requires *case management.*

• *Case management* focuses on the individual patient and his or her unique health care needs. Patients who benefit most from case management are high-risk, medically complex individuals (approximately 20 percent of the total inpatient population). These patients frequently have numerous comorbid conditions and are unlikely to follow a standardized approach to care delivery. Due to the complexity of their illness or state of health, they are at risk for adverse outcomes from both a clinical and a financial perspective. It is this high-risk population that benefits from individual case management.

Choosing an Appropriate Model

Early in the program design process, it was determined that a two-pronged approach to a care management system was needed: an acute care program and also a community-based case management program. (See figure 5-2.)

Acute Care For the acute care setting, the task force greatly appreciated the model developed by Karen Zander and the

Figure 5-2. Two-Pronged Approach to Care Management

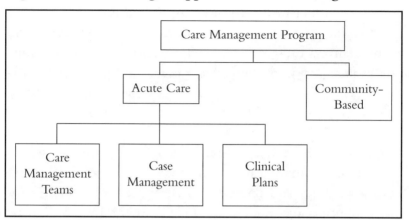

Center for Nursing Case Management. This model allows the primary care nurse to expand his or her role across unit boundaries. The case manager is a direct-care provider (while the patient is on his or her unit), but also case manages a select group of patients throughout the entire hospitalization (regardless of nursing unit). The task force had one major concern with this model: Would the case managers be effective in case managing a group of patients (across all nursing units) and also be able to handle direct patient care responsibilities?

The clinical staff and nurse managers on the task force felt strongly that to increase the likelihood of success, a model must be used that freed the case managers from direct patient care responsibilities. Thus, the case manager role at LGH was designed around accountability for achieving desired patient care outcomes for a subpopulation of high-risk patients. The case manager follows the patient closely from admission to discharge, regardless of the nursing unit the patient may be transferred to. The acute care program consists of three major components:

1. Care management teams (specialty-based)
2. Case management for the high-risk patient population
3. Standardized tools (clinical plans, protocols, management guidelines)

Note that *clinical plan* is the term used at LGH, which is synonymous with critical path or pathway. This is a framework or grid that identifies key interventions and outcomes that should occur against a timeline. It is used concurrently to plan, monitor, evaluate, and communicate patient care progress. Retrospectively, it is used for aggregate outcome measurement, variance reporting, and performance improvement.

Care Management Teams   Care management teams are physician-led, interdisciplinary care teams that include representation from all settings and disciplines that affect the outcomes for that patient population. For instance the neurology care management team is led by a neurologist and facilitated by the neurology case manager. The team also includes a representative from the following areas:

- Medical staff (including neurology, EMD, internal medicine, radiology, and cardiology)
- Home Health Services
- Social work
- Physical therapy (inpatient and outpatient)
- Nursing Representatives (from EMD, neuro-trauma ICU, and the neurology nursing unit)
- Rehabilitation unit
- QI department
- Dietary
- Hospital administration
- Pharmacy

Other team members that may be included on the care management team (based on the patient population) include representation from the Operating Room, Anesthesia, Wellness Center, Behavioral Health, Family Health Medicine, Infectious Disease, Geriatric Services, Diabetes Rehabilitation, lab, SNF, or physician offices.

Instead of looking at individual cases, the teams focus on groups of similar patients and their collective health care needs and outcomes. Care management teams monitor the effectiveness of the care being provided and design changes and processes to enhance patient outcomes, quality, satisfaction, and efficiency. These teams do not limit their focus to the quality of care during a patient's hospital stay, but also examine how to improve quality before, during, and after a patient enters the system. Currently, 20 care management teams are in place. (See figure 5-3.)

These teams provide a framework for the continuous improvement of the care being provided and ensure appropriate and cost-effective use of resources for that patient population. They are responsible for developing tools to better manage the patient population (such as critical paths, protocols, management guidelines, and so on) and make modifications in the recommended plan of care based on actual patient outcome data and trends. The goal for using these standardized tools and guidelines is not to endorse "cookbook medicine" but, rather, to promote implementation of best practices.

Inpatient Case Management Inpatient case management focuses on the high-risk, medically complex patient population. Frequently, these patients are the elderly and chronically ill who have multiple pathophysiologies and are unlikely to follow a

Figure 5-3. Current Care Management Teams

• Cardiology	• Neurology	• Primary Care– Community
• Cardiothoracic Surgery	• Neurosurgery	• Psychiatry
• EMD	• OB-GYN	• Pulmonary
• General Surgery	• Oncology- Hematology	• Rehabilitation
• Gastroenterology	• Orthopedics	• Trauma
• Neonatal	• Pediatrics	• Urology
• Nephrology		• Vascular

standard path. Ideally, they are identified on admission and referred to a case manager. The case manager then works closely with the physicians, nursing staff, and family to facilitate and coordinate the care of the patient throughout the episode of illness.

Standardized Tools   Clinical practice standards help to identify the best way for providing care to a given patient population. Using resource and clinical outcome data, the care management teams are able to assess current practice patterns and identify opportunities to improve outcomes and reduce inefficiencies.

The LGH care management teams developed clinical plans (with associated standardized physician orders) for approximately 50 of the highest-volume diagnoses and procedures. Built on the critical path methodology, it is a user-friendly strategy for capturing current practice patterns as applied to a defined predictable patient population. The clinical plans serve as a guidepost to care without dictating how care is to be given and incorporate expected clinical outcomes rather than focusing only on tasks and activities. The outcome of a five-day discharge is broken down, and daily outcomes or event outcomes are incorporated into the clinical plan. If there is a variance or an expected outcome is not achieved, the variance is documented and an action plan is developed to get the patient back "on the path." This variance tracking process allows for concurrent quality improvement, as well as retrospective outcome measurement. These outcome data can be incorporated into subsequent revisions of the clinical plan, which then becomes an even more reliable tool for current practice.

Clinical plans are a permanent part of the patient's medical record and help to manage and document the patient's progress through an episode of illness. Several of the clinical plans extend across the continuum of care into rehab, subacute care, and home care. Patient and family clinical plans are also available for each clinical plan. These plans are more patient-oriented, but still allow the patient and family to have a detailed view of what is planned. These have been found to be extremely effective as both education and communication tools.

Other tools developed by the care management team members include nursing protocols, medical guidelines, and disease management guidelines. These tools represent an attempt to better manage a diagnosis or treatment from both a cost and a quality perspective.

Predicted Outcomes and Staffing Requirements   To accurately predict the necessary staffing and potential benefit of the acute care management program, key outcomes (that the program could affect) needed to be identified and quantified. These were then used to calculate the number of inpatient case manager positions needed (and in what specialties). Variables that were considered included:

- Volume of cases
- Average cost per case
- Average profit/loss
- Average length of stay (LOS)
- Number of outliers (greater than two standard deviations) for LOS or cost
- Comparisons to benchmarks

A hospital profile (in a spreadsheet format) was created to quantify the impact that the care management system might have. This profile identified the top 50 diagnosis-related groups (DRGs) by volume, average cost per case, and average profit/loss. It also showed the variance between the average LOS at LGH and a national benchmark. Two benchmarks were used for this profile: Health Care Financing Administration (using the lowest LOS for the mean range) and the Milliman & Robertson LOS (using its inpatient utilization model for a moderately well managed delivery system).[4]

To determine the potential cost savings that might be realized, the following assumption was made: A population-based approach to care management (through the development of critical paths, guidelines, and so on) and case management of high-risk patients would achieve a reduction in the average LOS for a minimum of one-third of the targeted patient volume. This reduction would be equivalent to the variance between current LOS and benchmark LOS.

The total cost savings by DRG was then calculated by taking 33 percent of the total volume of cases within each targeted DRG and multiplying that by the LOS variance from the benchmark. For example, if a specified DRG had a volume of 900 per year with an actual LOS of 5.5 days, and if the DRG benchmark LOS is 4.0 days, the variance between the actual and benchmark LOS would be 1.5 days. Based on this assumption, it would be anticipated that care management could reduce the LOS for approximately 300 patients by 1.5 days (for a total potential reduction of 450 patient care days).

The number of reduced hospital days was then multiplied by the average cost per day to determine the total cost savings attributed to LOS reductions per DRG. To make this prediction as realistic as possible, the average cost per day that was used in the calculation was the average cost per day for the last two days of the hospitalization. Because frequently the largest percentage of patient care costs are accrued at the beginning of the hospitalization (which would not change despite total LOS reductions), this provided a more realistic and predictable estimate of the impact of LOS reductions.

DRGs and medical specialties that demonstrated the most opportunities for improvement were those with high volumes (a small improvement could equate to significant total cost savings) and also those that had large variances from the benchmark.

It was recognized that other opportunities for improvement existed beyond LOS and cost reductions. These included: improved clinical outcomes and patient satisfaction, reduced resource utilization, earlier discharge planning, standardization of pharmaceuticals and supplies, and improved patient care coordination and patient flow. The level of detailed analysis that would be required to quantify these opportunities was not carried out in the planning process, but was later evaluated by each of the care management teams once they were established.

Based on the above hospital profile (and potential LOS reductions), the number of case managers by specialty was determined. The data supported the creation of 10 case manager positions (for a total of 9 full-time equivalents [FTEs]), including:

- Cardiology: 3 FTEs (the hospital profile identified cardiology as the largest single opportunity for cost reductions due to the high volume of cases)
- Orthopedics/neurosurgery: 1 FTE
- Trauma: 1 FTE
- Neonatal/pediatrics: 1 FTE
- Surgery: 1 FTE (includes general surgery, vascular surgery, and urology)
- General medicine: 1 FTE (neurology and GI)
- Oncology: .5 FTE
- Pulmonary: .5 FTE

The case manager positions were budget neutral and existing, budgeted FTEs were used. Nursing managers and directors provided the necessary 9 FTEs to the Care Management Department from vacant RN positions. A bachelor's degree in nursing or a related health care field was established as the minimum educational requirement for these positions.

Community-Based Case Management   The community-based case management program was created to target the patient population within the community that is at high risk for illness exacerbation and costly readmissions to the acute care setting. These are often the frail elderly and chronically ill. Frequently, hospital administrators wait to develop continuum-based case management until there are financial imperatives to do so. Increased management of risk frequently

substantiates the need for such a community case management program. At LGH in 1995, there were no financial
imperatives to decrease the number of admissions (reimbursement was based on admissions). The prime motivator was the
belief that a case management program for the chronically ill
and elderly within the community (focusing on health promotion and symptom management) was the best strategy to
improve outcomes.

The community case management model was created parallel to the inpatient model. (See figure 5-4.) Its mission is to
foster independence and enhance the quality of life for individuals and their families within the community who are at
risk of illness exacerbation. (See figure 5-5.) This is achieved
by enabling them to participate in their own course of treatment and by facilitating access to supportive mechanisms and
available services.

**Figure 5-4. Community Case Management Model:
Conceptual Framework**

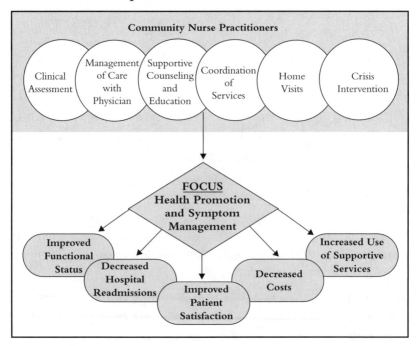

Figure 5-5. Criteria and Potential Diagnoses of High-Risk Patient Populations

Criteria	Potential Diagnoses
• Chronic illness	• CHF
• Decreased support systems	• COPD/Asthma
• >2 unscheduled hospital admissions/1 year	• Pyelonephritis
	• Sudden death survivors
• Repeated use of EMD	• Diabetes with complications
• High risk of exacerbation of chronic illness	• AIDS
	• Cellulitis
• Does not qualify for home health services	• CVA/neuromuscular disease

The conceptual framework for community case management demonstrates that the expected outcomes of the program include:

- Improved functional status of the client as measured by the SF-36 tool
- Decreased hospital readmissions
- Improved patient satisfaction
- Decreased costs
- Increased use of supportive services (both LHA and community services)

Community-based management contributes to the health of the community in the following ways:

- It detects and fulfills unmet medical and social needs.
- It provides home visits and advances clinical assessment.
- It decreases fragmentation of care.
- It identifies and mobilizes effective community services.
- It facilitates cost and resource management so that either cost avoidance, cost-effectiveness, or efficiency is achieved.
- It enhances primary care access.

- It improves communication of patient needs between the acute care and community settings.
- It advances integrated community health promotion programs.
- It assists in developing ambulatory disease management guidelines.
- It allows for increased productivity of primary care physicians.

Community case management is provided by two nurse practitioners (NPs) working collaboratively with the patient's primary care physician to facilitate early identification and treatment of symptom exacerbation. Their patients are primarily covered by Medicare. The largest percentage of the referrals to the program are from the primary care physicians within the Lancaster General Medical Group and VNA (patients who are no longer home bound or have no further skilled care needs). (See flow chart in figure 5-6.) Congestive heart failure is the most common diagnosis for referral. Each NP manages a caseload of approximately 25 to 30 patients.

Department of Care Management

The LGH care management proposal (which included both the acute care and community-based programs) was accepted by the LGH board of directors, and in February 1996, the Department of Care Management was created. The program development and design for the Care Management Program took approximately 12 months to complete. Other program elements detailed in the proposal included:

- Case manager role definition, requirements, and job description
- Case identification and screening process to determine appropriate patients for case management
- Care management teams' role, responsibilities, and membership

- Management structure (the position of director of care management was created and reports to the senior vice president of patient care services for the Alliance)
- Educational process for case managers
- Implementation timeline and communication plan (for hospital staff, physicians, and patients)
- Budget

Figure 5-6. Referral Process

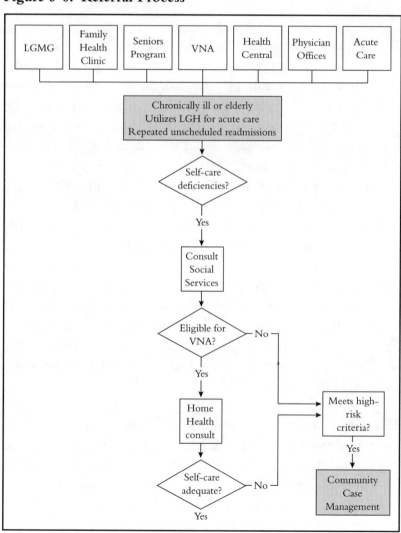

- Process flow for critical path development and modification
- Variance analysis and outcome measurement reporting process

Implementation of the Care Management Program

Program implementation focused heavily on recruiting and educating case managers, establishing the care management teams (discussed earlier), and obtaining physician participation and buy-in.

Recruiting Qualified Case Managers   All initial acute care case manager positions were filled with internal candidates. Internal recruitment provided the opportunity to find individuals who consistently demonstrated a positive attitude and had been successful in using a team approach for problem solving. The disadvantage was that no one had any prior experience in the case manager role.

The case manager role calls for an assertive individual who is self-motivated, enjoys autonomy, and has strong clinical experience in the specialty, strong organizational and time management skills, and the ability to communicate extremely well (and diplomatically). Individuals who are likely to become frustrated (and thus less likely to be successful) are those who lack a commitment to patient advocacy, have difficulty with collaboration, need a structured environment that focuses on task completion, believe that cost containment cannot be achieved without sacrificing quality, and have difficulty looking at the "big picture."

Educating the Case Managers   For a new role and a newly created department, orientation and education can be the biggest challenges. Although all the case manager positions have core requirements and expectations, case managers had to develop their unique role based on the specific needs of their patient population and their team.

Obtaining Physician Participation and Buy-In   Physicians play a central role in shifting the model of care from a fragmented, episodic style of care delivery to the systematic approach of care management. Within that framework, the goal is increased standardization toward best practices, more predictable outcomes, and reduced resource utilization. Physicians' actions account for 75 to 80 percent of health care resource utilization.

The most successful strategy in changing physician behaviors was clearly demonstrated within the care management teams. Change for its own sake is not the goal of the teams, nor is it pure cost reductions. The goal of every care management team is to improve patient care and outcomes. Improved efficiencies, appropriate resource utilization, and reduced costs are the secondary benefits. By providing the physicians with reliable data on their current practice patterns and variations, the associated costs for providing care, and patient outcomes, the teams became active partners in the performance improvement initiatives.

Evaluation of the Care Management Program

Most hospitals are challenged by the search for the most effective method for measuring how the care that is provided affects the outcomes. Important data elements include current practice patterns, the community standard, best practice recommendations from the research literature, and national benchmarking comparisons. The ideal method for establishing and achieving meaningful, quantifiable outcomes is difficult to determine. The results experienced by the care management program at LGH have been very positive. Figure 5-7 shows some of the selected outcome indicators classified into four major categories: quality of care, efficiency of care, customer satisfaction, and quality-of-life and functional status.

Trends demonstrate that the LGH patient population is older and sicker (as defined by average severity group).

Despite that, based on the indicators shown in figure 5-7, LGH demonstrated the following:

- Reduced unscheduled readmissions within 30 days
- Reduced LOS in both the Medicare and non-Medicare populations
- Improved patient satisfaction (as measured by Press-Ganey)
- Reduced average adjusted cost per case

Figure 5-7. Selected Outcome Indicators, by Category

Quality of Care

- Mortality
- EMD visits postdischarge
- Readmissions (within 30 days)
- Pharmaceutical appropriateness
- Clinical plan variances
- Patient safety/falls
- Complications
- Unplanned return to ICU
- Pain management
- Blood utilization
- Medication errors
- Infection rate

Efficiency of Care

- Average LOS (compared to benchmark)
- Average cost/case (excluding outliers)*
- Number of cost or LOS outliers
- Number of ICU days (severity adjusted)
- Delays in discharge
- Percent of UM reimbursement denials
- Clinical plan variances
- Preprocedure LOS
- Delays in procedure start times
- Unit/department productivity indicators

Customer Satisfaction

- Patient/family satisfaction survey scores (Press-Ganey)
- Patient/family letters
- Physician and employee surveys
- Discharge planning implementation tool

Quality-of-Life and Functional Status (SF 36)

- Physical functioning
- Role limitations (due to physical problems)
- Social functioning
- Bodily pain
- General mental health
- Role limitations (due to emotional problems)
- Vitality
- General health perceptions

An outlier is defined as two standard deviations from the mean.

- Severity-adjusted LOS below the expected LOS at a statistically significant level (P value ≤ 0.01)
- Increased compliance with evidence-based guidelines (as measured by clinical plan and guideline variances)
- Increased discharge planning (as measured by earlier identification of discharge needs and increased number of appropriate referrals)
- Decreased severity-adjusted mortality compared to expected (statistically significant at a 0.01 level)
- Increased compliance with the hospitalwide patient aggregation plan
- Reduction in primary C-section rates (consistently below the national average)
- Reduced blood utilization for targeted surgical case types
- Reduced percentage of LOS outliers
- Achievement of individual Care Management Team objectives and specialty-specific outcome indicators

Limitations of Outcome Evaluation

The goal of case management is to provide the best possible care in the most efficient and effective manner. Improvements in care and subsequent outcomes can be difficult to quantify, and it is often impossible to prove any correlation between the action and the outcome. Numerous variables may influence the results, including patient-specific factors that cannot be controlled for. If a new clinical plan is implemented and LOS drops significantly, is the change in LOS truly related to the clinical plan? It is likely to be a factor, but is only one of many variables that can influence LOS. Several limitations of outcome measurement include:

- A small number of "outliers" can significantly influence the "average" of case profiles.
- As current short stay hospitalizations (one- to two-day LOSs) are transitioned into the outpatient setting, the average LOS for the remaining inpatients is likely to rise.

- Frequently, several factors or initiatives are influencing cost reductions and improved outcomes. Except in an experimental research design, cause and effect will not be able to be established.
- As inpatient populations change, severity adjustments of outcomes become more critical.
- Interval changes to the cost accounting structure/standards can (and will continue to) affect data analysis and accurate trending.
- Determination of the outcome indicators that are the most sensitive may not be established for several years into a program. No statistical tests are currently feasible for accurately predicting potential cost reductions because the patient populations are continually changing.

Population Profiles as a Method for Presenting Clinical Outcome Data

Population profiles are frequently the ideal method for presenting clinical outcome data. By creating a template of the various levels of analysis, the profiles can be readily updated and individualized to provide a valid comparative analysis. Population profiles provide a methodology to:

- Compare trends within your institution
- Compare performance with benchmark (internal or external)
- Provide peer group comparisons
- Demonstrate practice variations
- Establish realistic goals and set priorities
- Provide a monitoring tool for performance improvement initiatives
- Foster accountability
- Flag potential problems
- Negotiate more favorable contracts
- Assist in "predicting" or identifying potential trends

To support outcome trending for the care management department, seven levels of patient population profiles were created. These included:

1. *Top 25 DRGs based on volume and cost:* This level of report looks at key hospital indicators, such as ranking by volume and cost, average cost per case and LOS comparisons for two years, benchmark LOS (M&R LOS for a well-managed delivery system), variance from benchmark, and average profit/loss. Using this hospitalwide profile, it is very easy to readily identify the top volume and/or cost DRGs and also the DRGs with the highest variance from benchmark.

2. *Care management team DRGs:* This level of report looks at only the DRGs that are associated with each specialty care management team. DRG-specific outcomes that are reported include volumes, average cost per case and LOS comparisons, LOS variance from benchmark, and average variable direct cost per case comparisons. In addition, comparisons are made using the combined DRGs for that care management team. Although a team may be focusing on improving outcomes for one specific DRG, such improvements frequently result in improved outcomes for the entire specialty population.

3. *Department-level DRG analysis:* This report identifies the top procedures and diagnoses by volume and cost for a specific department (such as general surgery). Procedure/diagnosis-specific outcomes show trends related to volumes, average cost per case and LOS comparisons, and key clinical indicators such as mortality, unexpected returns to the OR, infection rate, major complication, swan ganz catheter utilization, OR minutes, and so on.

4. *Physician peer group comparisons:* This report is specific to an individual procedure or diagnosis. It compares physician groups or individual physicians to each other and to the

hospital mean. The indicators that are compared include trends related to volumes, average cost per case and LOS comparisons (adjusted for severity), charges by department (EMD, OR, anesthesia, pharmacy, ICU, radiology, cardiology, and so on), and key clinical indicators such as mortality, unexpected returns to the ICU, infection rate, complications, blood utilization, and so on.

5. *Individual physician practices:* This report is specific to an individual physician practice providing data related to top-volume DRGs or procedures, average cost and LOS trends, and benchmark LOS comparisons. Other outcome indicators are provided based on specialty and specific performance improvement initiatives.

6. *Daily cost/resource utilization profile:* This report is specific to an individual procedure or diagnosis. It provides costs by department for each day of hospitalization. This puts detail into resource utilization for each day and helps to identify opportunities for improvement (from a clinical as well as a financial aspect). For example, if the last two days of hospitalization consist of only a room charge and oral medications (no therapies or treatments), one must consider whether an alternative site of care might be appropriate. The report also indicates on which day referrals were made for services such as social work, physical therapy, home care, and so on to better identify discharge planning opportunities.

7. *Primary care inpatient analysis:* This report is specific to primary care physician groups. It includes volumes as the attending physician group and primary care physician, LOS and cost by DRG with comparisons to the hospital mean, referring physician groups by volume, payer source trends, average costs by department (cardiology, pharmacy, lab, and radiology), and total cost of EMD visits that did not require admission. Other primary care practice indicators include: percent of weekend discharges, percent of

admissions with a severity score of 0–1, number of hospital days denied by payer, percent of low-birth-weight deliveries, number of NICU admissions, number of pediatric admits for asthma, number of LOS outliers, and percent of readmissions within 31 days.

Subsequent Care Management Initiatives and the Next Phase

Approximately one year after implementation of the care management program, the following case manager FTEs were added to the Care Management Department:

- 2 FTEs for trauma case manager positions (due to demonstrated outcomes and value)
- .5 FTEs for neurology to make a 1.0 FTE position (based on new stroke treatments options and development of the Stroke Center at LGH)
- 1.0 FTE for a rehabilitation case manager position
- .5 FTEs for a psychiatry case manager position

These additional FTEs were provided by each specific service line or specialty and were based on demonstrated outcomes and/or clearly identified opportunities.

Other initiatives that have promoted effective care management across the continuum include:

- Implementation of an Ambulatory Diabetes-State Management Program
- Integration of care management and the Department of Social Work, Utilization Management, and Quality Improvement
- Development of population and physician practice profiles
- Development of an advanced CHF disease management program

- Utilization of functional status evaluations (SF 36) for 10 case types (baseline, three-month, and six-month evaluations obtained)
- Redesign of the roles and processes for providing utilization management
- Development of ambulatory disease management programs for diabetes, CHF, asthma, and anticoagulation
- Pilot of a Medical Call Center for demand management
- Value Enhancement Initiative utilizing national benchmarking data with 10 care management teams

The next phase of care management is to create an Alliance-wide care management system. This population-based health management system will extend beyond institutional boundaries. This strategic plan for a systemwide care management approach, serving as an integrating mechanism for patient care, is to be completed in 1999.

Conclusion

Most hospitals are challenged by the search for the most efficient and effective method for redesigning patient care delivery. Utilization of clinical paths to coordinate patient care was frequently an early response to this challenge. Critical path utilization has subsequently evolved into a more sophisticated model of care management that includes interdisciplinary collaboration, standards for best practice, benchmarking, population profiling, case management of high-risk individuals (both in the acute care setting and the community), and longitudinal outcome analysis.

The care management program at LGH is viewed by senior management as the method for implementing strategic planning and goals. This view has facilitated the overwhelming acceptance, success, and growth of the program. Within an integrated health system, care management has the potential to be a vehicle for cost containment in the delivery of comprehensive, high-quality health care services throughout the system.

Interdisciplinary care management teams are at the center of the process for performance improvement. They bring the key individuals to the same table to determine the best way to provide care to a given patient population. Their goal is to create a process for determining, monitoring, and controlling care that facilitates optimal clinical outcomes. This is achieved by developing relationships among the medical staff, multidisciplinary care providers, and hospital administration to improve the quality and efficiency of care provided to patients while reducing costs.

The other key component for the care management teams is outcome management. Data must be provided to the teams. Clinical practice is not dictated to the physicians or any members of the clinical team (administrative edicts rarely work). Rather, data representing improved clinical results are powerful incentives.

References

1. *100 Top Hospitals: Benchmarks for Success, 1997* (HCIA Inc., Baltimore, MD, and William M. Mercer, Inc., New York, 1997).

2. J. Burns and M. Sipkoff, *1997/1998 Hospital Strategies in Managed Care* (New York: Faulkner and Gray, 1997), pp. 195–203.

3. Lancaster Health Partnership, *Lancaster County Health Profile* (1997).

4. Milliman & Robertson, Inc., *Healthcare Management Guidelines,* 1995.

CHAPTER SIX

Creating High Performance through Quality Improvement

Mary Nolan, RN, MS

Albany Medical Center Hospital (AMCH) is a 650-bed tertiary care hospital and part of Albany Medical Center, an academic medical center with a medical college and faculty practice in New York. This case study discusses the hospital's journey to improved performance, which occurred in two phases: operational performance improvement and clinical performance improvement. It also describes the components and implementation of its patient-centered care model and identifies many of the results of the change.

Impetus for Change

By the end of 1990, AMCH was faced with a financial crisis that threatened its survival. The reasons for the crisis included the impact of the New York State reimbursement system, long lengths of stay (LOS), closed beds, impediments to patient access, and high resource utilization. When efforts at cost

117

reduction and an initiative to obtain relief through state funding failed to solve the crisis, the organization decided to make a series of leadership choices to improve performance through the use of total quality management (TQM) and team principles. The initial goal of achieving financial stability soon gave way to a drive to improve the delivery of patient care and core clinical processes.

The path to high performance occurred in two phases. The first (operational) phase consisted of building leadership, using systematic planning to get results, learning to use data and information to measure performance, and improving operational performance. Leaders in the organization learned to work together as a team to get results. The three major areas of emphasis for improvement during this period were financial turnaround, correction of multiple issues within the nursing department, and overall leadership development. During this phase, it became evident that in health care individuals do not work in isolation and that a team-based approach was essential to success.

The second (clinical) phase began with a commitment to make partnering and teamwork the dominant methods for getting the work done. The focus of TQM, accepted as the process for performance improvement, was shifted from financial to clinical areas. The organization began a restructuring process aimed at supporting quality initiatives, which resulted in improvements in both service-line clinical programs and the entire patient care delivery system.

It was understood that the initial commitment to change and improvement had to be embraced by both physicians and staff. Performance improvement was seen as a continuum, from incremental improvement of an existing process to complete redesign of the process. The extreme end of the continuum was reengineering, with radical changes in how work was done. Leadership's role became one of mapping the way—coaching team members to be self-directed, high performing, and focused on the goals.

Phase 1. Developing Capability for Operational Performance Improvement

In December 1990, a senior leader with over 25 years' experience at AMCH was appointed hospital director and given comprehensive responsibility and authority to set the hospital on a new course. He immediately formed the Hospital Operations Senior Leadership Team, including a new vice president of nursing. Although all members of the team had been at AMCH before this time, some, including the new nursing executive, were promoted to new roles within the team. The hospital director immediately set a clear direction for the institution, transforming the leadership style from a reactive to a proactive mode in order to respond rapidly to meet emerging requirements of the health care environment. Leaders from within were expected to make the change and commit to a new way of managing the organization.

Achieving a Financial Turnaround

The AMCH operations team started the change process by shifting from a fragmented "silo" approach to decision making to a shared decision-making approach for solving the institution's financial problems. The hospital director appointed the vice president of nursing and the director of laboratories to jointly lead the team's cost reduction effort with an annualized target of $15 million. The vice president of finance made it clear that all cost reductions and revenue plans were to be realistic and accurate. Both the hospital director and the vice president of finance knew that success required rigorous precision in all aspects of financial management and that this discipline needed to begin immediately.

The operations team met at least every other day during the last two weeks of December with the expectation of meeting the target without negatively affecting either care or revenue. The team decided to use an assessment system that involved looking at the impact of budget cuts across the organization. Potential action was prioritized based on two factors: its impact on the delivery of care and the ability to implement it.

Initially, everyone on the team was expected to identify potential cost reductions without an absolute target or quota and to look creatively for potential innovative changes. Conflict and old behaviors did not disappear at once, but slowly a new way of working together emerged during this process. The target reduction was achieved collaboratively.

This collaborative approach to financial management has proved to be successful as the organization continues to cycle through cost reductions. Significantly, important and necessary capital improvements have not been sacrificed in the process. In 1992, a new inpatient facility was opened and equipped with the latest in clinical technology. These successes served as a powerful reinforcement of the new process. The effectiveness of setting goals, planning actions, and solving problems as a team was undeniable. The larger community also took note of the new mode of leadership and its impact on both the hospital and the citizens of the region.

Slowly but surely a new culture was emerging, one in which patients came first and high-quality care was the priority, with a foundation of financial stability. Leadership now knew that with a commitment to change coupled with sustained effort, it was possible to improve. Although a natural resistance to change surfaced in the early stages, it was transformed into positive energy through communication, education, and involvement. Everyone had to let go of the view that the problems were someone else's fault. Everyone learned that it takes continuous hard work to be proactive and good at what you do. The payoff was sustained success.

Restructuring the Nursing Division

Many of the underlying causes of the financial difficulties were related to nursing division problems, as evidenced by closed beds and the prevalent use of outside agency staff. There was significant variation in how care was delivered, and systems for nursing standards, staffing and resource management, problem solving, and decision making were inconsistently applied. Every service within the division used different management approaches. The annual staffing budget was based on history and competition for resources rather than on objective patient care requirements. There was no centralized, automated system for monitoring nursing hours or quality indicators for nursing care. Not surprisingly, staff morale was low and turnover high. Although nursing leaders worked together when a major situational crisis occurred, on a day-to-day basis they still worked in their departmental silos. The new vice president of nursing formed a nursing management team charged with improving the delivery of patient care within existing financial constraints. Team members quickly understood that action was needed to break down departmental barriers and build a cohesive, productive nursing care delivery system.

Developing a New Process for Making Decisions   Restructuring in the first week of 1991 created a new Division of Nursing focused on the development of management systems for the nursing care delivery system. The new structure was announced at the first meeting of the vice president of nursing and the entire nursing management team. The vice president of nursing had been part of the "mess" and needed to quickly demonstrate to the group that she could execute change. Three key principles for performance were introduced at this meeting and became consistent themes for nursing improvement:

1. Covey's *The Seven Habits of Highly Effective People* was discussed, with an emphasis on the importance of using one's energy on matters that can be influenced rather than focusing on concerns that are not in one's circle of influence.[1] The two circles were particularly helpful given the

nature of patient care. Often staff and managers were over-whelmed by complex interdependencies of clinical care and voiced a sense of powerlessness to "fix it all." Covey's circles clearly demonstrated the need to separate what we can do within our role or job versus tackling the entire problem. The circles were used repeatedly over the next year to remind everyone where to invest time, energy, and resources.

2. Decisions would be made by consensus, which meant find-ing solutions that everyone could support, even if they were not everyone's first choice. Leaders would not leave a team meeting saying, "I don't know what they were thinking when they made that decision." Consensus decisions began to be made in an environment of trust where participants were willing to speak up and learn to select the best out of multiple solutions for problems.

3. The leadership group made a commitment to become a high-performance team.

Use of these performance principles began at that first meet-ing when a prior decision to implement a new comprehensive system for standards was revisited. A number of individuals, particularly nurse managers, expressed concern about how this could be accomplished in light of the many problems facing nursing. The nurse executive called on the group to explore the pros and cons of the proposed comprehensive standards system, review alternatives, and discuss the implementation process. After discussion, the group decided unanimously to support the decision to implement the new system, which was consistently supported from then on. This was a crucial deci-sion point because it started the nursing organization on a journey to consistent standards of care and systems across all nursing departments.

Mapping Out Long-Range Plans for Improvement   The group then developed a map of long-range plans for improvement with the needed actions and responsible persons clearly spelled out. It was at this juncture that we began to experience significant and important change. One area that needed to be addressed was the management of staffing issues. Previously, delivered nursing hours had not been documented, and use of local, outside agency staff was prevalent, particularly in the adult units. Subjective war stories about staffing abounded with little or no objective data to verify the facts. Thus, it was essential to stabilize staffing to ensure buy-in and to create trust among the nursing leaders and staff. The first staffing intervention was to use outside agency traveling nurses, who were selected by the managers and were willing to commit to at least three months' service on a unit. With this length of service, leaders and staff could plan on stable staffing and validate that the needed competencies were in place. Cost for this approach was minimized by negotiating favorable contracts with the traveling nurses agencies.

The second staffing intervention was to commit to the minimum number of hours needed for safe nursing care. The first time the vice president of nursing actually was able to get a realistic view of the actual hours delivered was when she personally input the paid worked hours from the paid full-time-equivalent (FTE) reports into a Lotus spreadsheet program. These hours were backed into nursing hours by using formulas that calculated average hours available based on the average daily census. Nonproductive time such as orientation could not be identified; nonetheless, the areas that had critical staffing shortages were identified immediately. Most were in the medical division. The director of nursing for the medical units was given authority to hire to meet safe staffing levels (mutually agreed-on nursing hours) even if the resultant FTEs exceeded budgeted levels. This intervention was essential to establish stable staffing and was key to communicating nursing leadership's commitment to safe patient care. The nurses on the affected units began to trust their leaders again. Within the year, both the high and low nursing hours were managed successfully.

This logical approach to staffing and patient access was based on a flexible, realistic system, not just on numbers on paper that were not tied to reality. The payoff was tangible: all beds were reopened.

From 1991 to 1993, the Division of Nursing implemented numerous policies and procedures for ensuring consistency and logic in nurse staffing, based on a primary nursing philosophy, including the following:

- A model for staffing standards
- A patient acuity system that allowed for benchmarking and external comparisons
- A systematic approach to budgeting for nursing hours
- A consistent system for managing daily staffing with both minimum and maximum staffing standards based on patient acuity and workload standards
- Systems for planning and implementing changes

An outside consultant provided essential management information to the nursing management team, focusing on problem solving and situational leadership. A patient-centered reorganization of the nursing division was implemented, which resulted in a reduction in management positions. The shared governance model was redesigned and implemented based on the principles of Porter-O'Grady.[2] These changes were intended to drive nursing care improvement through involvement and empowerment of the staff.

Effecting Changes in Leadership Style   Gradually, an essential shift in leadership style began to occur among the nursing leaders. They migrated from exhibiting reactive, crisis-oriented, competitive, and even fearful behaviors to being a cohesive, patient-centered team that was accountable and used information, consensus building, and goals to create change. A continuous focus on priorities that the nursing management team could influence, rather than the areas of concern that were not within their influence, was important to the shift. The long-range plan enumerated the annual goals and kept the team centered and productive. With this approach, it was easy to discern when the team was getting off track, and we could quickly employ strategies for righting our course.

Leadership expectations were made clear. The entire nursing management team had "shot-in-the-arm" days with the management development consultant. This provided objective, external feedback on progress. As initiatives were completed and results actualized (for example, expanding the cardiac surgery program, increasing OR utilization, or opening a bone marrow transplant program), energy and spirit were rebuilt. One of the indicators of success during this time was the improvement in nursing scores on the Press-Ganey Patient Satisfaction Survey. Scores rose from the 30th percentile ranking to the 65th percentile. Other accomplishments included the elimination of external agency staff and the opening of all beds with adequate staffing.

Developing Mechanisms for Coping with Change The many gains in nursing were highly visible in 1993, but there had also been losses. The changes were begun with a commitment by the entire management team, but not all leaders were able to meet the new expectations. Some felt that this new way of doing business was not for them and they left the management team. In June 1993, a nursing retreat was held for the management team to "let go" and prepare to move on to the next stage. The first day was at a retreat center in an Adirondack Mountains setting. The following "lessons from geese" were used to allow the team to pause and reflect on the stages and impact of the many changes we had experienced:

- As each bird flaps its wings, it creates an uplift for the bird following. By flying in a V formation, the whole flock adds 71 percent more flying range than if each bird flew alone. *Lesson 1:* People who share a common direction and sense of community can get where they are going more quickly and easily because they are traveling on the thrust of one another.

- Whenever a goose falls out of formation, it suddenly feels the drag and resistance of trying to fly alone and quickly gets back into formation to take advantage of the lifting power of the bird immediately in front. *Lesson 2:* If we have as much sense as geese, we will join in formation with those who are headed where we want to go (and be willing to accept their help as well as extend help to others).
- When the lead goose gets tired, it rotates back into the formation and another goose flies up to the point position. *Lesson 3:* It pays to take turns doing the hard tasks and sharing leadership.
- Geese in formation honk from behind to encourage those up front to keep up their speed. *Lesson 4:* We need to make sure our honking from behind is encouraging—and not something else.
- When a goose gets sick, wounded, or shot down, two geese drop out of formation and follow their fellow member down to help and protect it. They stay with it until it is able to fly again or dies. Then they launch out on their own, with another formation, or catch up with the flock. *Lesson 5:* If we have as much sense as geese, we too will stand by each other in difficult times as well as when we are strong.[3]

The stress of multiple change initiatives and the grieving associated with the loss of colleagues were explored and validated. Participants said what they needed to say, cried if they needed to, then let go of the past. We reflected on how we might be more supportive of each other in the future.

The other major activity at the retreat was the initial development of the team competency and empowerment flowchart. (See figure 6-1.) Briefly, the flowchart defines the necessary elements and cyclic relationships that undergird the outcomes associated with excellent patient care, high-performing teams,

Figure 6-1. Team Competency and Empowerment to Deliver Excellent Patient-Centered Care by a High-Performing Patient Care Team

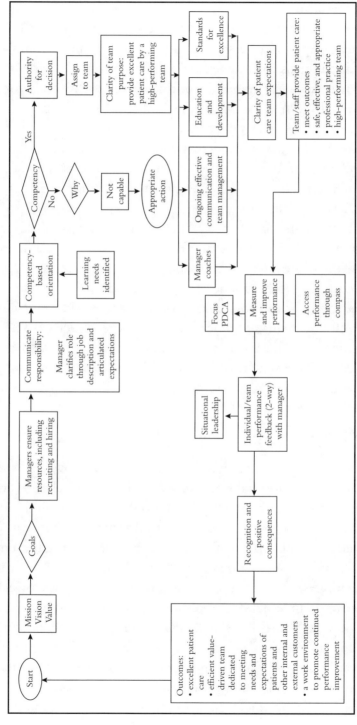

Reprinted, with permission, from Albany Medical Center Patient-Centered Care Manual/Generic Structure Manual published by Albany Medical Center, © 1996.

and continuous performance improvement. The steps include the recruitment of individuals; competency-based orientation; delegation of responsibility, authority, and accountability to individuals for a specific job; integration into a team; performance measurement; continuous improvement through Focus PDCA (Plan, Do, Check, Act);[4] and a focus on outcomes. These steps continually recycle and clearly outline the multiple factors needed to make the system function effectively. This relational map continues to provide guidance to staff and leaders in their quest for an outstanding patient-care delivery system.

Humor and fun were also important elements of the retreat. Everyone learned to do the "electric slide," and a "name everyone's favorite cartoon" contest was held. The second day was held at the hospital. The closure and high point of the retreat was the marshmallow pelting of the vice president of nursing by all the managers coordinated by the directors. The vice president of finance heard the noisy laughter, walked in, and became the new target for the pelting. Happily, he had a sense of humor and marshmallows do not stick!

Developing Expectations for Hospital Leadership

The hospital director led the development of overall expectations for the hospital leadership. He began with clear goals and did not waiver from the expectation that they would be met. These expectations/goals were specific targets with dates and related business plans if indicated. Examples of achievements included increasing cardiac surgeries from 1200 to 1600, opening a secure inpatient unit for Department of Corrections inmates, implementing an outpatient observation and infusion center, reducing LOS, and many similar goals. His commitment and persistence were coupled with an ability to actively listen, assess situations, and modify goals based on data and appropriate indications. His style created a positive and constructive environment that allowed leaders to grow and develop.

Detailed leadership expectations, consistent with a team-based approach and an emphasis on results, were communicated to all leadership staff. The expectations were included in position performance evaluation criteria and also used to develop managers. Gradually, defensive and other unproductive behaviors diminished. Everyone, including the hospital director, worked on improving relationships and teamwork. The necessity of this process was continuous because the overall health care environment contains multiple threats that can threaten the effectiveness of teams.

Measurement of gross results occurred only during this early phase. The primary indicators used were monthly financial reports for cost centers, overall financial performance, admissions, LOS, and Press-Ganey patient satisfaction scores. All of these improved during this phase: cost and LOS went down, while admissions, revenue, and patient satisfaction scores went up.

Phase 2. Developing Capability for Clinical Performance Improvement

Improving operational performance was only the beginning. Attaining high performance as a health care organization required maximizing gains through clinical improvement. It was evident that the successful interplay of all of the care disciplines and care functions was essential. However, accelerated improvement required effective integration that seemed impossible given the existing organizational structure.

Key structural reorganization changes were made to accelerate the improvement curve. A patient-centered system was created that incorporated both service-line and patient care delivery principles, maintained leadership accountability, and allowed for the maintenance of operational standards and performance. The goal of the reorganization was to break down the structural silos while facilitating the creation of a system that supported a service-line approach. The core business of patient care was emphasized, with financial stability and infra-structure support to the care mission as essential but sec-ondary objectives. The restructuring integrated management and patient care processes throughout the hospital, creating an environment that supported redesign and reengineering. The structure was flattened with fewer than four layers between the staff and the hospital director. This original restructuring has continued to evolve with better alignment with the service lines and improved effectiveness of the care delivery system.

Leadership within this new structure was of critical impor-tance. The vice president of nursing position was changed to the group vice president for patient care (GVPPC) position and made responsible for all of the clinical services delivered by nonphysician staff in the hospital. The vice president for medical affairs, the medical director, and the GVPPC formed a partnership to lead improvement in all aspects of patient care. The vice president of finance position was changed to the position of group vice president for the resource and support services, with responsibility for managing and improving the systems that provided resources and support to the patient care function. The two group vice presidents were joint leaders for the hospital operations team and were held accountable for quality, service, and cost/performance improvements by the hospital director.

Physician leadership for clinical performance improvement was integral to success. An associate medical director with expertise in clinical performance improvement was recruited to lead and foster quality initiatives, including clinical pathways and clinical process improvement.

The clinical services of the hospital were distributed across five different divisions prior to the reorganization. The divi-sions did not share similar priorities, and organizational barriers impeded communication and collaboration toward consistent patient care goals. To correct this, one patient care division was created with seven services organized according to the care delivered and the alignment with service/product lines. The new patient care organization was the key to breaking down silos and improving clinical processes to achieve high-quality patient care. The message emphasized was that everyone in the hospital was there to "serve the patient." The organization chart has changed frequently as restructuring and reengineering, dictated by a commitment to quality improvement, continue to evolve.

Service-Line Improvement

The hospital director realized that stand-alone budget reductions provided only short-term fixes to the financial challenges we faced. He believed that to survive in the long term, organizations must focus on cost-effective, high-quality care and that all members of the staff had to share a commitment to that vision. Hence, it was time to involve the staff who were at the point of service and doing the work.

The core principles of TQM were to be the center of AMCH performance improvement, including redesign and reengineering, based on the belief that if rework and waste were eliminated and processes improved, cost containment and reduction would follow. A quality-of-care system and structure were created to support clinical performance improvement and patient care redesign. The Hospital Quality Council was transformed to the Patient Care Quality Council and chaired by the hospital director. His involvement and leadership (at the council level) sent a significant message of commitment to the goal of quality improvement as a core value of the organization.

Service quality improvement teams were implemented with a focus on clinical performance improvement. Core process teams, such as documentation, medication administration, and patient care delivery were established for areas that needed ongoing improvement. Limited-purpose teams were established that focused on a specific problem process, such as registration, and ended when the work was completed. Figure 6-2 displays the structure for the quality system. After the process and structures for performance improvement were clarified, a quality education curriculum was established and training initiated throughout the organization.

The focus on clinical performance improvement took the form of two questions: What does the patient need, given a specific clinical diagnosis and problem identification (the processes and continuum of care related to a specific clinical service/program), and how does the patient receive the care (the care delivery system)?

The clinical processes provided through specific clinical service lines were improved through three major changes:

- Clinical pathways
- Service quality improvement teams
- Case management

Physician involvement and leadership were integral to success, particularly for clinical pathways and the work of the service quality improvement teams.

Figure 6-2. Quality Structure

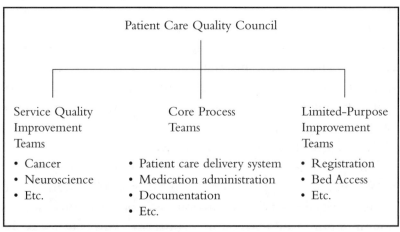

Reprinted, with permission, from Albany Medical Center Patient-Centered Care Manual/Generic Structure Manual *published by Albany Medical Center,* © *1996.*

Clinical Pathways A template for clinical pathways was created based on research of the literature and consultation with experts. The implementation of nursing standards and protocols also provided a foundation for pathway development. The associate medical director and a project coordinator (an RN with strong clinical, leadership, and analytical ability) facilitated each of the pathway teams. Due to its volume and cost, cardiac surgery was selected for the first pathway. A cardiac surgeon served as the leader of an interdisciplinary team. Systematic clinical data and evidence-based outcomes supported the pathway, which was successfully implemented. Ongoing variance tracking has driven numerous improvements in processes, including a decrease in days' waiting for cardiac rehabilitation, significant reductions in blood gas numbers, and improved protocols for anesthesia and postoperative recovery.

More than 28 pathways have been implemented since the first in 1994, resulting in many improvements in clinical care of patients and a more than 25 percent decrease in LOS. Meanwhile, patient satisfaction scores have been maintained.

Service Quality Improvement Teams Service quality improvement teams are interdisciplinary teams led by the physician chief of the service and a nursing leader working with specific patient populations. They focus on improving clinical processes and outcomes, and team leadership provides the operational linkage for defined pathway improvement implementation. The work of the transplant team is an example of the model's success. Participation in an external benchmarking study demonstrated that our program had excellent clinical results, but with an LOS and case costs that were greater than the other 15 institutions in the study. The internal team used the ideas and information from the study to change its practice patterns and processes. For example, it began discharging patients earlier and administering some drugs on an outpatient basis. Excellent patient outcomes were maintained while cutting LOS in half, saving between

$5,000 to $10,000 per case, with a total savings of $700,000 annually.

Case Management The third component in service-line improvement was the redesign of discharge planning and utilization management into the case management department. The staff changed from unit-based assigned discharge planners to service-line assignments as case managers, allowing patients to be followed from admission to discharge. The newly created role focuses on resolving issues that cannot be easily managed by the patient's primary nurse, who is accountable for managing the predictable plan of care and routine discharge planning. Such problems usually translate into additional inpatient days. Approximately 30 to 40 percent of the patients at AMCH fall into this category. Case managers also analyze data and act as resources for the service quality improvement teams. The case management system amplifies the efforts to reduce LOS while maintaining outcome goals for all patients.

Patient Care Delivery System Improvement

In 1994, the patient-centered care project was initiated with the defined purpose of ensuring that "care is delivered in a manner that assures that the patient is at the center of what we do and why we do it." Its goals and principles were similar to many patient-focused care redesign projects across the country. However, they were not compelling enough to persuade the nursing staff of the need to change the system. Fear among the nursing staff was rampant as they read about and heard many news stories about downsizing, job cuts, and unsafe care conditions as a result of redesign.

At the end of 1994, an interdisciplinary team of patient care staff and leaders evaluated the current nursing care delivery system. The GVPPC served as the team's leader. The group used TQM tools to construct flowcharts, collect data, and analyze care delivery. System findings included the following:

- Staff roles and the system varied by unit and by shifts within units.
- Staff assumed that they had to complete assignments alone and did not ask for assistance even when it was available.
- Nursing hours included nonlicensed staff already, but these staff members were not consistently trained nor were they used effectively.
- Patients frequently waited in a time loop for care because of handoffs among providers and lack of a team approach.

As a result of the multiple problems identified, the doubts in the nursing staff's minds regarding the need for change were resolved. All agreed that the system needed to be redesigned.

The original task force, with the addition of more direct-care staff, was transformed into the Unit-Based Clinical Model Design Team, fondly known as the "template team." This team was also led by the GVPPC, with facilitation by the quality management director. An adaptation of Ackoff's interactive planning process was used for the redesign process.[5] The interactive planning process takes a team through the following phases:

- Assessment of the current state
- Creation of an ideal design that is constrained to reality
- Completion of a gap analysis between current state and ideal design
- Identification of the targeted changes and the means and resources needed to achieve them—creating a work plan
- Implementation and evaluation

This team produced a template for the delivery of care that is used by each of the units that has implemented the system. The members also served as champions and leaders of the change process as units began to plan and implement the changes. Several "enablers"—strategies to assist this team to become internal experts and advocates for the system—were put in place. As a result, team members became competent in redesign, adding to the capability of the organization. These enablers included the following:

1. *The team was freed for two weeks to begin the redesign process.* During this time, team members received education on patient care redesign, performance improvement, and measurement; completed the assessment of the care delivery system; and began to create the new model. A team from another hospital that had already implemented redesign met with the team and shared the benefits and challenges of the new models of care. Humor and fun were used to ease the burden during this intensive two weeks (for example, mock beach days and games). This two weeks' freedom from normal routines and activities energized team members and released their creativity, starting the staff on a journey of changing their beliefs and behaviors to make the future changes possible.

2. *The team was part of developing every element of the model.* Team members worked for 10 months, from May 1995 to February 1996, and created a new model for delivering care on the inpatient units. The Patient-Centered Care System consisted of four elements: patient expectations, collaboration, environment, and outcomes. As a result of this involvement, team members were able to advocate for every change that this new system created.

3. *The team tested the new direct-care delivery model with simulations on several inpatient units.* Team members wanted to create a team-based system that was truly centered on the patient and fostered collaboration rather than a hierarchical approach to care delivery. To do this, the roles of the team needed to be well understood and defined. The simulations provided a way to test both the team principles that were being developed and the roles. They tested all the direct-care roles, including the patient care associate, the new unlicensed direct-care position, and the patient support associate (PSA) role, a multifunctional role that

included dietary, housekeeping, equipment and unit cleaning, transportation activities, bed making, answering lights, and other comfort measures for patients.

The simulations were done on the two units that were to be the first adopters of the system, and team members took on a variety of roles. The first two patient support associates roles were assumed by the director of the laundry and a night shift nursing supervisor; and a nurse manager and RN were patient care associates. Significant learning occurred, including a better understanding of what it is like to work in another's role. The simulations made it possible to assess the team's effectiveness and gave insight into the type of education needed to develop a team-based system. The simulations were repeated until the system was fine-tuned and the template team was able to validate that it worked better than the existing system.

4. *The team was able to make changes across a number of arenas.* Team members identified the need for additional patient equipment and furniture on the units as a result of evaluating the environment. They developed a plan within certain financial parameters ($250,000) that was approved and implemented. This reinforced their ability to get something done. They also proposed a nursing ministation (a patient care center built into the walls in the corridors) to contain medications, linens, small supplies, IV materials, and other equipment. It was created to bring the staff closer to the patients and support the team system. One of the impediments the team had to conquer was a directive from the hospital director that plant renovations were not possible. Thus, team members prepared a series of plans and a presentation to justify the need for the centers. Their success was a living illustration that the point-of-service staff was empowered to influence the organization's decisions and that the organization was willing to invest in changes to improve the delivery system. The patient care centers have been a major success.

5. *The team was not designing specifically for its unit.* Team members developed a general best-practice model to be used by unit design teams in applying the principles, system changes, and best practices of patient-centered care to their particular unit. This allowed the template team to be objective in its assessment and planning. The first two units to implement the design had an RN staff member on the template team, and each became a co-leader of her unit's design team. This linked the implementation teams to the expertise and support that had been developed in the template team. The nurse manager was the other co-leader for each unit, creating a partnering between staff and management.

These five strategies created an environment that empowered this team to create a new inpatient care delivery system that is patient centered. A description of essential components of this new model follows.

Components of the Patient–Centered Care Model

The new patient-centered care system had two essential components: patient expectations and the patient care team system.

Patient Expectations

Eight expectations of AMCH patients and family/significant others as seen "through the patient's eyes" were defined to ensure that the patient care team system would be centered on the patient. These expectations are based on the priorities identified through the AMCH hospital patient satisfaction measurements, patient and family/significant other feedback, other quality measures, and Picker Institute research on patients' needs and concerns. They include the following:

- Patients being treated as individuals
- Coordination and integration of care
- Information, communication, and education
- Physical comfort
- Emotional support and alleviation of fear and anxiety
- Involvement of family and friends
- Transition and continuity
- Clean, cheerful patient and work environment[6]

These eight expectations were considered in every aspect of the new team-based care delivery system design and are continually measured through the Press-Ganey patient satisfaction tool.

Patient Care Team System

The core of the unit-based redesign is the Patient Care Team (PCT) System. The PCT is defined as a consistent group of competent staff with a shared, 24-hour a day responsibility for patient care and services for a defined patient cluster. Team members collaborate through common performance goals, complementary skills, and a common approach to work. They hold themselves mutually accountable and affirm each other's contributions for the team's results and outcomes.[7]

A high-performing PCT has clear responsibility, authority, and accountability and works in a learning environment that provides the respect, trust, and support needed to develop the following attributes: shared leadership, shared responsibility, alignment of purpose, effective communication, focus on the future, focus on process and results, valuing creativity and diversity, and rapid response. These attributes were chosen based on the work of the template team. Bucholz and Roth's model most closely matched the desired characteristics and provided a system that was used as a basis for team education and development.[8] A unit cultural assessment tool was selected to measure the staff's progress in becoming team oriented.

Questions from the tool were aligned with each attribute and are the basis for evaluating team performance and staff satisfaction. Other tools are used to measure patient satisfaction, clinical indicators, progress toward high performance as a team, and overall staff satisfaction with the work environment.

Development of the model was a challenge. The issues brought out in the assessment were not fully resolved in models seen in other organizations. One of the most important issues the team wanted to address was the staff's "loner" approach to the delivery of care. It was believed that this was pivotal to improving the system. Finally, the patient care team was created, as pictured in figure 6-3. Each team has at least two RNs. This provides a partner for the professional responsibilities and immediately breaks down the tendency to function alone. The other care partners are either licensed or unlicensed direct-care staff. In most cases, they are licensed practical nurses (LPNs) or patient care associates (formerly nursing assistants). A team of two RNs will usually have one care partner. On the day shift from 8 A.M. to 5 P.M., the other member of the care team is the patient support associate (PSA), who fulfills the multifunctional role mentioned earlier for dietary, housekeeping, transportation, and comfort measures for patients. Another key issue was creating a system in

Figure 6-3. Patient Care Team

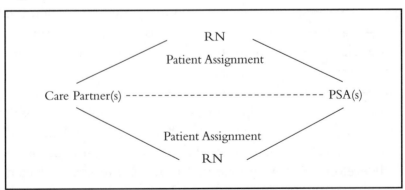

Reprinted, with permission, from Albany Medical Center Patient-Centered Care Manual/Generic Structure Manual *published by Albany Medical Center,* © *1996.*

which staff have enough time to meet patients' direct-care needs. This is a key indicator on a quality-of-worklife tool used for measurement.

The number and skill mix of a PCT is based on patient requirements over a 24-hour period. These requirements were determined by activity studies and tested in simulations on each unit as they were implemented. The team is assigned to a cluster of patients within a circumscribed area for at least a three-month period. The complete team for a cluster of patients includes all the team members across all the shifts. A 24-hour focus is expected for providing care, and each member of the team shares responsibility and workload rather than just focusing on his or her specific assignment. Consistency in expectations for primary nursing and the professional responsibilities of the RN were also clarified and reinforced.

Implementation of the New System

Important strategies were identified to build staff capability to make the significant changes in culture and systems required in the redesign. Key human resource issues needed to be addressed before implementation was started. These included communication, transition, education, and competency planning for the transition. Training in these areas prepared staff to apply the design through unit implementation of the patient-centered model.

Communication

Awareness was raised early in general staff meetings and other informal venues. Special staff meetings to describe the system and implementation plan were held as the first two units began to plan implementation. The staff members on the template team conducted these meetings. Just prior to the meetings, the Real Nurse initiative in New York State had evoked concerns in some of the staff about the impact of redesign. The Real

Nurse initiative was a public information campaign to communicate concern to potential patients about use of unlicensed staff in hospitals, with the basic message that every patient deserves a real nurse. AMCH staff knew that we were working on redesign of the care delivery system and were concerned about facing some of the issues raised. The direct communication from staff to staff was very effective in reducing these concerns. Communication continued on a regular basis in many ways, including staff meetings, newsletters, bulletin boards, and so on. Most important was direct, open communication with staff. The final resolution of these concerns came as unit staff actually became involved on unit design teams and began to assess their units and implement the model. They discovered that they had the ability to influence the implementation and saw that the primary aim was to improve the delivery of care on their unit.

Transition

Work redesign evokes fear of job loss among staff. Often this is fueled by media reports about the current health care environment, including the potential loss of jobs as a result of hospital restructuring or downsizing. The institution made the commitment that no one would lose his or her job as a result of the redesign initiative. A plan was developed to retrain staff to meet the expectations of the new roles, particularly for the patient care associates and patient support associates. In addition, a redeployment plan was put in place for staff who could not meet the new expectations. These plans worked well and the transition was smooth.

Education

Several educational programs were developed to support different aspects of the program. Orientation and training curricula were developed for all the roles. Core education programs were developed for each step of the redesign journey and included:

- *Patient-Centered Care (PCC) core education:* "Conditioning and Training" were given to all staff to provide basic knowledge as the redesign process was started and the unit team was appointed.
- *PCC start up:* "Going Out for the Team" was the initial, day-long program that helped the unit design team get started.
- *PCC RN education:* "Coaches' Training" was the class for RNs on the role changes created by PCC, including leadership, supervision, delegation, and assignment.
- *Team building:* "Time for the Major League" was a two-day, team-building course for all staff based on the team model. The 24-hour team for a specific cluster was relieved to attend this course to assist staff in developing the skills needed for a team-based system.

Competency Planning

One of the most difficult challenges in planning was to ensure that an adequate number of competent staff were available as units implemented patient-centered care. A number of changes occurred in how orientation is completed, and many improvements occurred in the overall system for developing competency. Figure 6-4 is a flowchart of the competency process. Gaps and problems in the systems that existed prior to the PCC initiative stood out once the redesign process began. The result has been overall improvement in the competency of all staff when they complete orientation, not just the staff in new roles.

Unit Implementation

Each unit had a design team that had representation from every role and shift on the unit. Each team was launched with

Figure 6-4. Competency Process Flowchart

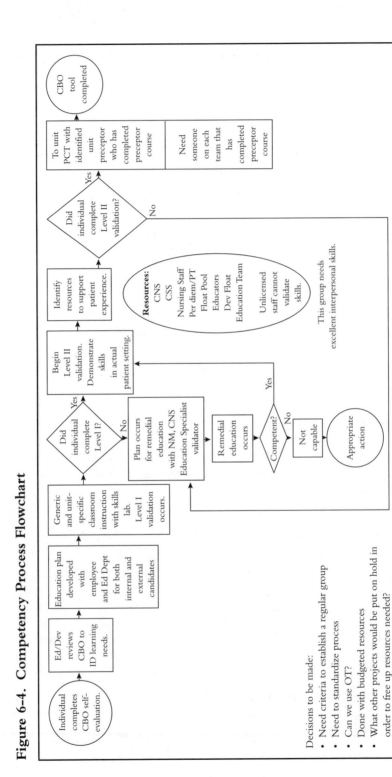

Decisions to be made:
- Need criteria to establish a regular group
- Need to standardize process
- Can we use OT?
- Done with budgeted resources
- What other projects would be put on hold in order to free up resources needed?

Reprinted, with permission, from Albany Medical Center Patient-Centered Care Manual/Generic Structure Manual published by Albany Medical Center, © 1996.

two days of education and then met for full days every one to two weeks. A manual was developed by the template team to document the design and provide a working document for the unit-based teams to implement PCC. The companion to this manual was a well-developed template work plan, which served as an implementation guide for the unit-based design teams. Activity studies were done by all units and other patient care staff who provided direct care to patients on the units. This provided a database for units to use in their design process.

Use of Simulations in the Template Work Plan

One essential step in the work plan was the use of simulations. Each unit simulated the application of the model to its unit before fully implementing the model. An evaluation tool was used for both simulation and implementation to monitor improvement. The simulations tested the proposed staffing pattern and gave the staff an opportunity to learn the system before it was fully implemented. Problems identified during the simulation were resolved by the design team before complete implementation. Each unit had a milestone meeting to review the implementation plan, new staffing pattern, and financial modeling, and to confirm readiness for implementation with key stakeholders (for example, the GVPPC and patient care service director).

Partnering and team principles were used in planning for implementation and rollout. A rollout plan identified the phases and dates of implementation for each unit. The two medical-surgical units, selected as first implementers, initiated implementation planning at the same time. The two design teams were educated together and shared ideas and concerns throughout the process. Each of the first two unit design teams had RNs from a unit that was next on the rollout plan. This continued for all of the units and gave unit staff experience in redesign before their unit actually began redesign implementation.

This partnering principle, built into the rollout plan, assisted in rapidly engaging a larger number of staff in the redesign process and also reduced fears about the process. This built momentum to move forward, and units were actually asking to begin planning as soon as possible. Eight units were implemented in a 12-month period.

Implementation of this system took a significant effort and needs regular reinforcement and improvement. Team member relationship building is a constant challenge for the staff and managers. The lessons from the geese have been used to help units deal with the impact of the changes. The unit design teams are transformed to unit "work teams" after implementation, using shared governance principles. The work team continues to focus on the performance of the team system by monitoring the unit score cards (discussed in the next section), deciding on opportunities for improvement, and planning to ensure continuing cycles of improvement at the unit level.

Evaluation of Unit Performance

Each unit developed a balanced scorecard that incorporates the quality, satisfaction, and cost indicators listed in figure 6-5. The unit monitors its performance over time. The first goal is to maintain performance while going through the change process. All of the units maintained their indicators within the original control limits during implementation. Improvements are occurring in the units that first implemented change. In one unit, the overall patient satisfaction score rose from 87.70 to 90.00 in the first quarter after implementation—the highest score the unit ever achieved. It has continued to rise and was 91.30 a year after implementation. In addition, significant improvement has been seen in the quality-of-worklife score for staffs' perception of whether they have enough time to provide for patients' direct-care needs on the first two units. It rose from 3.25 before implementation to 4.47 after implementation, a 38 percent improvement. (The highest possible score is 5.00.) The salary dollars per patient day were less than in the two years before implementation. Other units are showing similar improvements. It is expected that it will take a year for the system to settle into place in each unit, and improvement in the indicators is expected to continue as this occurs. The overall nursing score for all units on the patient satisfaction survey has risen from 87.5 to 89.3.

Figure 6-5. Patient-Centered Care Measurements

Unit Measurement	Patient Measurement	Team Measurement
Performance:*	*Performance:*	*Performance:*
Quality of care 7-3	Care and treatment well	Shared leadership
Quality of care 3-11	coordinated	Shared responsibility
Quality of care 11-7	Staff sensitivity to	Aligned on purpose
Promptness responding	inconvenience	Future focused
to call button		
Medical error rate		
(# errors/meds		
dispensed)		
Unit fall rate		
(# falls/pt day)		
Function:	*Function:*	*Process:*
Hospital's concern not	How well your pain was	Focused on process and
to discharge too	controlled	results
soon	Advice you were given	Values, creativity, and
Adequate information	on caring for yourself	diversity
regarding patient		Rapid response time
rights		Effective communication
Cost:	*Cost:*	*Cost:*
Cost per patient day	Average length of stay	(Salary dollars) financial
(CPPD) vs. redesign		modeling
CPPD		
Satisfaction:	*Satisfaction:*	*Satisfaction:*
Likelihood of recom-	Daily cleaning	Quality of worklife
mending facility	Overall cheerfulness of	study
	hospital	
	Information given to	
	family	

*Nosocomial infections and skin breakdown are monitored through hospitalwide programs.

Reprinted, with permission, from Albany Medical Center Patient-Centered Care Manual/Generic Structure Manual published by Albany Medical Center, © 1996.

Patient response to the team system has been overwhelmingly positive. Patients continually praise both the team system and staff in all of the roles on the patient satisfaction questionnaire. Many patients have done something special for the staff on a unit. In one case, a patient made an "E 4 Excellence" plaque for the staff on one of the first units, using the unit floor designation (E4) creatively. All the units have had some type of positive feedback from patients and families about the team system through letters, comments on the patient satisfaction surveys, and in-person feedback.

The staff's response in the first two units has been even more striking. They are vocal in saying that this is the best thing that AMCH has ever done. They also expect problems to be resolved. The manager for one of the units compares today with the past: "Before we did patient-centered care, the staff would complain and expect nothing to happen. Now, they either take care of it themselves and let me know or, if it's something that they need me to help with, they expect me to get it done with them."

Results

The care delivery redesign realized the significant challenge of creating high performance through a team-based system. An ongoing need exists to continually develop competency and skills, manage relationships, and reinforce the cycles of improvement. Both managers and staff continue to develop as a team and as individuals with improvement as their ongoing aim. Taking TQM and making it work at the point of service is an effective, but difficult, road to high performance. However, after you get there, it is worth the effort.

AMCH persisted in sustaining clarity of purpose, commitment, comprehensive effort over time, and involvement to create capability for high performance using team and TQM principles. They have seen major results. The hospital turned the bottom line around from a $7 million loss in 1990 to over a $2 million positive margin in 1991, and has continued to improve its financial results since then, with more than a $7 million margin in 1997. Admissions have increased almost every year since 1991. LOS has decreased more than 25 percent between 1994 and 1997 to 6.3 and is continuing to decline. The score for "likelihood to recommend the hospital" is the overall key indicator for patient satisfaction, and has consistently improved (from 87.5 to 88.7) during the same period that LOS decreased. The hospital also participated in a productivity benchmarking study of approximately 40 similar institutions during this time and was the top performer in the study.

An external signpost of the success of the ongoing changes that have ensued is designation as a "Top 100 Hospital" in 1994, 1997, and 1998, identifying AMCH as a top performer nationally. The analysis that is the basis for this designation encompasses clinical, financial, and other indicators in the Medicare database. Other external quality awards and recognition have been received, such as inclusion in the *U.S. News and World Report* annual list for specific programs (urology and cardiology) in 1996 and 1997. The hospital and faculty practice also received a JCAHO score of 97 with no Type I recommendations in 1998.

Conclusion

AMCH was forced to rapidly improve its performance when financial instability put its survival at risk. This change process began with survival as the goal but quickly shifted to a vision of high-quality patient care. Clear purpose, commitment to improvement, willingness to invest comprehensive effort over time, and involvement at all levels of the hospital made it possible for AMCH to build its capability for high performance.

There were two major phases in this journey for AMCH. The first focused on operational improvements. It began with a leader who was willing to set a new direction for the organization and truly change its culture. Clear expectations were set for the senior leadership team to shift from reactive to proactive management behaviors, work together as a team, and demonstrate the ability to achieve goals and expected results. The two major improvements during this phase were a financial and nursing turnaround that built the ability and confidence of the leadership team.

The hallmark of the second phase was a commitment to team and TQM principles/techniques as the way to continue this turnaround, with clinical performance improvement as the priority in the future. Straight cost reduction that is not based on changing the organization's clinical processes would put the mission and quality of the organization at risk. There was no doubt about the commitment to quality when the hospital was reorganized based on patient-centered principles. This allowed the breakdown of organizational silos that impeded clinical process improvement. The focus of the second phase was on improving clinical service lines and the patient care delivery system.

Clinical service lines were improved through clinical pathways, the work of service quality improvement teams using TQM tools and techniques, and case management. Work redesign was used to develop and implement a patient-centered, team-based system for delivering care. Measurable improvements have occurred across all elements of performance (quality, satisfaction, and cost) throughout both phases.

AMCH continues to build its capability for high performance. There is no end to the journey. The constant challenges and difficulties created by the state of the health care system necessitate the willingness to constantly question the current state and seek improvement. Clarity of purpose, commitment to improving performance, sustained effort, and involvement make this possible.

References

1. S. Covey, *The Seven Habits of Highly Effective People* (New York: Simon and Schuster, 1989).

2. T. Porter-O'Grady and C. K. Wilson, *The Leadership Revolution in Health Care: Altering Systems, Changing Behaviors* (Gaithersburg, MD: Aspen Publishers, 1995).

3. "What's Good for the Goose . . ." *Incentive* 169, no. 12 (December 1995): 47.

4. W. E. Deming, *Out of Crisis* (Cambridge, MA: MIT, 1986).

5. R. L. Ackoff, *Creating the Corporate Future* (New York: John Wiley & Sons, 1981).

6. M. Gerteis, S. Edgman-Levitan, J. Daley, and T. L. Delbanco, eds., *Through the Patient's Eyes: Understanding and Promoting Patient-Centered Care* (San Francisco: Jossey-Bass Publishers, 1993).

7. Adapted from J. R. Katzenbach and D. K. Smith, *The Wisdom of Teams: Creating the High Performance Organization* (Boston: Harvard Business School Press, 1993).

8. Adapted from S. Bucholz and T. Roth, *Creating the High Performance Team* (New York: John Wiley & Sons, 1987).

Bibliography

Andrews, H. A., L. M. Cook, J. M. Davidson, D. P. Schurman, E. W. Taylor, and R. H. Wensel, *Organizational Transformations in Health Care* (San Francisco: Jossey-Bass Publishers, 1994).

Blancett, S. S., and D. L. Flarey, *Reengineering Nursing and Health Care* (Gaithersburg, MD: Aspen Publishers, 1995).

Boos, M., ed., "Lessons from the Geese," *Agricultural Notes* 97, ELCA.

Griffith, J. R., V. K. Sahney, and R. A. Mohr, *Reengineering Health Care: Building on CQI* (Ann Arbor, MI: Health Administration Press, 1995).

Hammer, M., and J. Champy, *Reengineering the Corporation: A Manifesto for Business Revolution* (New York: Harper Collins Publishers, 1993).

Howard, J. M., and L. M. Miller, *Team Management: Creating Systems and Skills for a Team-Based Organization* (Atlanta, GA: Miller Howard Consulting Group, 1994).

Lathrop, J. P., *Restructuring Health Care: The Patient-Focused Paradigm* (San Francisco: Jossey-Bass Publishers, 1993).

Manion, J., W. Lorimer, and W. Leander, *Team-Based Health Care Organizations: Blueprint for Success* (Gaithersburg, MD: Aspen Publishers, 1996).

Orsburn, J. D., L. Moran, I. Musselwhite, J. H. Zenger, with C. Perrin, *Self-Directed Work Teams: The New American Challenge* (New York: Irwin Professional Publishing, 1990).

Uhlfelder, H. F., ed., *The Advanced Team Guide: Tools, Techniques, and Tips for Experienced Teams* (Atlanta, GA: Miller Howard Publishers, 1995).

Winer, M., and K. Ray, *Collaboration Handbook: Creating, Sustaining, and Enjoying the Journey* (Saint Paul, MN: Amherst H. Wilder Foundation, 1994).

Zenger, J. H., E. Musselwhite, K. Hurson, and C. Perrin. *Leading Teams: Mastering the New Role* (New York: Irwin Professional Publishing, 1994).

PART THREE

Lessons for the Future

CHAPTER SEVEN

Lessons Learned from the Case Study Redesign Initiatives

Mary E. Mancini, RN, MSN, CNA, FAAN

Despite their commonality, most health care facilities would argue that their specific mission, vision, history, culture, community needs, operating systems, and fiscal and human resources make them unique. Thus, they often find it difficult to replicate redesign programs that have been successfully implemented elsewhere. However, as the case studies in chapters 2 through 6 show, most redesign initiatives have common elements that can be applied to the redesign needs of different health care facilities. This chapter identifies and discusses eight common elements.

Eight Elements Common to Successful Redesign Initiatives

The case studies in chapter 2 through 6—the transition of a Veterans Affairs Medical Center to primary care in Washington, DC; the patient-centered redesign and differentiated practice model implemented at Gundersen Lutheran in La Crosse, Wisconsin; the integrated team project at Elmhurst Memorial

155

Hospital in Elmhurst, Illinois; the development of case management and care management programs at Lancaster General Hospital in Lancaster, Pennsylvania; and the effort to build high-performance teams at Albany Medical Center in New York—are examples of successful redesign programs. The challenge facing patient care administrators is that of drawing from these case studies those elements that are directly applicable to their situation or organization.

Following are eight common elements that can be viewed as a foundation for establishing a successful redesign initiative in any organization:

1. Recognizing the motivation for changing the status quo
2. Articulating a clear purpose and vision for the future
3. Having a leader with a strong, positive, personal reputation
4. Demonstrating collaboration and teamwork
5. Using a data-driven or evidence-based process
6. Demonstrating a willingness to invest in training
7. Developing an empowered workforce
8. Maintaining a comprehensive effort over time

Recognizing the Motivation for Changing the Status Quo

It has been said that the only person who likes change is a wet baby. Yet when we talk about change, we tend to discuss it as if it were a natural thing to do. Actually, the opposite is more often true. When developing organizational change processes, many institutions fail to consider the vast body of literature that exists on change theory. These writings provide valuable insight into components that differentiate successful from unsuccessful redesign strategies.

According to Lewin, an important component to consider when implementing change is the motivating factor.[1] He writes that for changes to be implemented successfully, there needs to be a sense of discomfort with the status quo and a

desire to make a change. It is the leader's responsibility to create the appropriate level of discomfort within the organization—
a level that serves to motivate the staff to change without
disheartening them.

Every day health care organizations attempt to make significant changes in their corporate culture and their operating systems. The successful ones take the time to specifically
address their motivating factors. The individual motivating
factor itself is not as important as the fact that it is identified
and the status quo recognized as a less than desirable state. In
so doing, those who long for the "good old days" before the
change process started begin to be seen as willing to accept
the unacceptable.

Albany Medical Center Hospital was absolutely clear that its
survival depended on change. Senior management was consistent in sending the message that change was not only necessary but desirable. The vice president of finance worked with
the vice president of nursing and the director of laboratories
to set realistic financial targets and was unequivocal that the
target of $15 million in reductions had to be met. Maintaining
current spending patterns was not an option, but neither was
compromising quality. In the same way, nursing leadership
articulated that the status quo, defined as low Press-Ganey
patient satisfaction scores and the use of external agency personnel, was no longer an acceptable state of affairs. When
placed within this context, resisting change was clearly a more
difficult stance to justify.

The Veteran Affairs Medical Center in Washington, DC
(VAMC), was equally specific in recognizing its motivating
factors. First, the VA headquarters had mandated that each
medical center develop an approach to managed care; and,
second, an increasing amount of data indicated that the
VAMC had cost, access, and continuity of care issues that
needed to be addressed. Leadership recognized these as motivating factors for change and, in a positive manner, exploited
them by using the factors to create a level of discomfort with

the status quo and a willingness to consider new and innovative approaches.

Achieving a level of discomfort with the status quo does not require as severe a threat to its survival as Albany felt. Nor does it take a mandate from an external source, as was the case with VAMC. Sometimes it occurs in more subtle ways, such as at Lancaster General Hospital. Lancaster was not under a financial imperative for change. Rather, leadership evaluated the institution's strengths and weaknesses in relation to its external market. They made a strategic decision to develop case management and care management, particularly as it applied to the elderly.

The important point in all the cases presented is that the current situation was no longer a desirable state for the institutions. As such, change began to be recognized as an opportunity, not just a threat.

Articulating a Clear Purpose and Vision for the Future

After the need for change is recognized and a sense of discomfort with the status quo exists, the next common element among organizations that redesign successfully is that they are able to articulate a clear purpose and vision for the future. This is where organizational mission and values seem to make a difference.

Shared Vision and Guiding Principles   Successful organizations are clear about their mission and vision. Staff at all levels are able to articulate the same set of values and operate in concert with them. "Shared vision" was the phrase used to describe this element in developing the integrated team approach for Elmhurst Memorial Hospital. This was articulated as the factor that "brought the team together." The belief at Gundersen Lutheran that patient care characteristics should drive the required nurse competencies set a specific point of reference that everyone could understand and act on.

The VAMC case study points out that before its redesign the lack of clarity around values allowed each service to interpret and develop its own values and mission statement as it deemed appropriate. Without a written mission statement or set of values, there was no unifying corporate culture regarding patients or patient care. Staff members could feel they were doing what they should, but in actuality they were often working at odds with one another. Addressing this void as part of any redesign process provides everyone—staff and patients—with a common point of reference and a measurement standard for changes as they are recommended and implemented.

The participants in the redesign at Gundersen Lutheran developed "principles" to guide them through their process. They saw them as their guideposts, stating that "often, when confusion abounded, these principles would be used to keep the task force on track so that members could focus on the main purpose and thrust of the work." One of the hallmarks of unsuccessful redesign projects is that they lack a clear set of written guidelines that staff can use as their touchstone during the transition. Without these, every participant is able to place his or her own personal "spin" on the motives and defining values of the undertaking. There is no agreed-on point of reference for discussion, action, or evaluation.

Passionate Commitment to the Project   The ability to effectively articulate a clear purpose and vision for the future requires passion. The coordinator of the redesign project—the champion or identified leader who advocates for the changes—must be filled with a burning desire to see the project through to completion. It would be difficult to find an example of a successful redesign initiative in which the person responsible for the project lacked passion for the program or commitment to the institution and its mission and vision. However, we all know of examples of organizational changes made by individuals who lacked a belief in the value of the changes they were asked to implement or who failed to see a direct link between the changes and the institution's mission. These redesigns are nearly always unsuccessful. The VAMC case study pointed out that the project coordinator's "belief in the project and ability to promote and sell the transition was extremely beneficial as she communicated the importance of the project throughout the medical center." In the same case study, "Because [the associate director for patient services] had a passion for the primary care model and its impact on patient care, she was able to guide and support all staff, some of whom were having difficulty with the vision and changes associated with primary care." These are the types of statements that are consistently found in case studies of successful redesign initiatives.

In evaluating any redesign initiative, it is important to analyze the depth and breadth of commitment to the program and the links between the program and the established mission and vision. Is there a clear champion for the program who believes in its value to the institution? Any redesign initiative that lacks at least a core group of individuals with this type of passionate commitment to the program will have a very low probability of success.

Having a Leader with a Strong, Positive, Personal Reputation

Having a vision for the future and a willingness to champion the change process with passionate conviction is not enough to ensure a successful redesign process. A leader also must have a positive, personal reputation within the organization. The nurse executives in the case studies all had solid reputations to draw on. They were viewed as effective leaders in their organizations. Their ability to influence went beyond the boundaries of the nursing department and was recognized throughout the organization. As such, they were given the opportunity to lead their facilities during times of great change.

Successful redesigns ultimately fall back to a sense of relationship. Someone once said that "relationships are not important things; they are everything!" When the status quo is being threatened or abolished, having a reputation as an effective leader will often provide the leader—acting as change agent—with that extra measure of acceptance from the participants that is necessary to achieve success. There will always be a sense of distrust when change is first presented. However, those individuals who have a reputation for honesty and for achieving results will be in the best position to lead effectively when fundamental changes, such as those associated with system redesign, are being implemented.

At the moment that major redesign efforts are being considered or implemented, it is not possible to build this type of positive reputation. However, if the identified leader of the process does not have the necessary credibility or reputation, all is not lost. In the case of Albany Medical Center's new nurse executive, her reputation as an effective leader was among the reasons she had been recruited to the position. She moved quickly to demonstrate that her reputation was deserved and she could be trusted.

Another alternative is to look for others in the organization who do possess the desired positive reputation. These individuals may or may not hold official managerial positions within the organization, but they are opinion leaders. It will increase the likelihood of success to ensure that these individuals have early buy-in or have active roles in the development of the project. As the Elmhurst Patient Care Services Team recognized, it was not the title of the individual alone that was the important factor for success. In this situation, it was his or her competence in interpersonal communication, problem solving, and the ability to articulate and advocate a personal vision that made the difference. These three characteristics are often cited as common to successful change agents.

It should be pointed out that because it is most often a high-visibility project with significant financial implications, work restructuring is the type of situation that can make or break the reputations of the key executives involved in the process. In some cases, even when restructuring is clearly in the organization's best interest, leaders may be unwilling to place their personal/professional future in jeopardy. In this unfortunate situation, the risk of failure overwhelms the opportunity for innovation.

Demonstrating Collaboration and Teamwork

Teamwork, multidisciplinary work teams, team players, team leaders—these phrases are sung like the Siren's chorus to Odysseus whenever work restructuring is discussed. They are included in nearly every article on redesign. As quoted by Michaels and Stull in their chapter on developing an integrated team at Elmhurst Memorial Hospital, "Health care is a team sport."[2] No other industry uses these team metaphors as often as health care does, and not without good reason. Yet what do these "team" phrases really mean? How are they implemented into successful redesign efforts? How does one move from rhetoric to reality? The case studies give some firsthand examples of collaboration and teamwork that help to crystallize the concepts.

The Elmhurst case study provides great insight into the current state of many health care organizations. The authors clearly define the fiefdoms or silos that still inhabit many institutions. Elmhurst demonstrated the ability to reorganize members from previously separated groups around the common title of Patient Care Services. However, developing the willingness to use a group-process approach and to seek each other out for problem solving was not instantaneous—it was a slow process with many starts and stops. The key to success was realizing the need to focus on the group process by teaching, role modeling, and mentoring those skills. As Michaels and Stulls stated, there always is a long road to trust that can be addressed only by specific attention and actions. Saying that everyone will work in a group and support one another is not good enough. Instead, it takes setting a clear expectation and then resocializing everyone to these new behaviors.

An interesting dimension of teams is the concept of involving all members of the team to the maximum amount possible in decisions that affect them. This lesson was pointed out in the case study from Gundersen Lutheran. The authors reflect on the problem they faced with their housekeepers and unit makers. They recognized that individuals in these jobs lacked buy-in and felt threatened by the development of the new role of patient service assistant. The lesson to be learned was that these individuals were not involved from the beginning of the discussion of role redesign because the focus was on the nursing staff. As the project evolved it was clear that the housekeeper and unit maker roles would change, too. Complicating the issue was the fact the housekeepers and the unit makers were under a collective bargaining agreement while nursing personnel were not. Some of these issues were eventually resolved by bringing a leader from the bargaining unit into the discussion. However, the situation might have been avoided if the group had been brought into the discussion at the beginning of the process.

In the case study from the VAMC, Hudec and Williams realized that focusing on the importance of teamwork would be something they would have addressed more specifically if they were to redo their project. They point out that they would have undertaken more research in the area of self-directed work teams before implementation. The authors felt that more group process work would have decreased some of the frustration they encountered in team development. This need was not limited to the staff members. It was also recognized at the level of the chiefs who needed guidance in developing their transformational leadership skills.

The Albany Medical Center Hospital case study provides some concrete examples of how teamwork should work at the executive level. Specifically, the authors point out that the leaders could not leave a leadership team meeting and say, "I don't know what they were thinking when they made that decision." Everyone was clear that it was their responsibility to speak up and question issues appropriately. Decisions were made by consensus based on what was best to meet the agreed-on mission and vision, not on personal preference.

The willingness to question leaders and other members of one's team is an essential attribute of effective teams. With group process, however, there is a danger that legitimate individual concerns that are counter to the groupthink will be discounted and pushed aside. All too often leadership meetings take on the atmosphere of the childhood story, "The Emperor's New Clothes." The process of groupthink can limit the willingness of individuals to question the prevailing thought process and individuals may become unwilling to express their true concerns or feelings.

This specific group dynamic is well described in the book, *The Abilene Paradox and Other Meditations on Management* by Harvey.[3] He explains how organizations frequently take actions in contradiction to what they really want to do. The inability to manage agreement is, he believes, a major source of organizational dysfunction. This is the type of situation that often leads to disastrous results, including the explosion of the space shuttle Challenger. In health care, the paradox is especially powerful between doctors and nurses, staff and management. If redesigns are to be successful, acknowledging and addressing this phenomenon is critical.

Effective leaders address this group dynamic head-on. Strategies include the following:

- Acknowledging the situation
- Pushing for clarity vis-à-vis any expressed concerns
- Exploring the potential downside of all decisions
- Avoiding the initial impulse to argue with or label the speaker as negative or lacking in commitment to the vision

Using a Data-Driven or Evidence-Based Process

Successful redesigns are data-driven or evidenced-based processes. Without a thorough review of the status quo and a plan for evaluating the effectiveness of the changes about to be undertaken, the result is often chaos. Changes are made indiscriminately—change for change's sake rather than change based on strategic analysis, an understanding of the process, and knowledge gained from reviewing the experiences of others. Organizational and system changes need to be based on a clear understanding of the individual institution's current realities and the specific targets for the future.

Historically, the staffing budgets at Albany Medical Center were based on prior-year allocations and competition for resources rather than patient care requirements. Simply decreasing costs without changing processes based on an understanding of the mission of the facility would, Albany's leadership staff believed, jeopardize their commitment to quality. Therefore, they recognized that their redesign process had to specifically address decision-making and measurement issues from the very beginning of the process. In addition, personnel and programmatic evaluation needed to be objective and applied in a consistent manner. By doing so, everyone understood the ground-rules for decision making and acted accordingly.

Another example of an evidence-based process is the development of the theoretical framework for change at Elmhurst Memorial Hospital. Its new organizational model for integrated teams was grounded in the works of Griffith, Sahney, and Mohr[4] and Ulschak and SnowAntle.[5] Elmhurst believes its commitment to building a sound theoretical foundation allowed it to avoid many costly mistakes that can occur when teams lack a common language and mechanisms for evaluation.

The impact of making decisions based on the evaluation of data is seen in all the case studies. Albany Medical Center provides an excellent example of linking an organization's beliefs directly to measurement criteria. In its redesign process, Albany recognized the importance of high staff satisfaction in achieving high patient satisfaction scores. To measure this key element of its model, which was based on the work of Bucholz and Roth,[6] Albany developed a tool to measure whether staff felt they had enough time to provide patient care and to get their general perceptions about the overall quality of work life. In doing so, the organization was able to directly link information on staff satisfaction to patient satisfaction levels.

Lancaster General Hospital used data throughout its redesign process. Specific data elements, such as volume of cases, average cost per case, and average length of stay (LOS), guided the development of staffing requirements and evaluated the effectiveness of changes. The use of benchmarking, with HCFA and Milliman & Robertson guidelines, was also recognized as significant to Lancaster's success. These external comparisons helped Lancaster establish reasonable targets for changes in LOS. Beyond LOS, Lancaster recognized the need to establish meaningful and quantifiable outcome measures. Therefore, outcome indicators were very specifically chosen in four major categories: quality of care, efficiency of care, customer satisfaction, and quality of life and functional status.

Gundersen Lutheran was successful in decentralizing infusion therapy based on a thorough assessment of patient care needs and the development of quality monitors and staff proficiency verification. The result was a cost-effective program without a decrease in quality. Failing this type of thorough assessment, simply looking at the cost of a centralized department could have led to a short-sighted decision to eliminate the infusion therapy department on the assumption that unit personnel would pick up its duties—an assumption that in many cases has proven false.

Demonstrating a Willingness to Invest in Training

Despite our desires to the contrary, internalizing a new culture or values, learning new skills, accepting new roles, or building new teams does not happen overnight. Significantly more time is needed for education than is anticipated. In the health care environment, a type of in-service education has been assumed to be effective in changing behavior. However, this short, isolated, didactic educational experience has not proven effective when dealing with substantive role or socialization issues. Role modeling, role-play, open discussion, and frequent repetition over a prolonged period of time appear to be needed to achieve significant and lasting change. As we have noticed with changes in the former USSR, people do not automatically understand how to use freedom. In health care, we assume we can tell health care professionals that they are empowered and give them a quick course in continuous quality improvement, and they will leap up to meet the challenge. This just does not seem to be the case.

Successful organizations are willing to invest in their employees and spend the time necessary to ensure that they are able to acquire these new skill sets. If members of an organization do not spend sufficient time discussing and evolving their own mental models in interactions with their leaders, conflicting and competing visions begin developing within the organization. Building teams is hard work. One must not assume that because professionals are involved in the process that teamwork will flow naturally. From the CEO to the employee just hired into an entry-level position in housekeeping, every employee must work on a daily basis to become and remain effective and efficient team members joined together around their common commitment to the mission and vision of the organization. Successful redesign efforts address these issues early on and build their redesign plans with sufficient time and fiscal resources dedicated to meeting the identified learning needs.

Training in Clinical Competency   A specific area of training that is critical in health care organizations is clinical competency. Skills that initially appear to be simple to teach are either not so easily taught or require more expert knowledge than anticipated. Many redesign efforts assume that unlicensed individuals can be quickly taught to do the "simple" tasks of phlebotomy, respiratory care functions, physical therapy support, or other basic nursing duties. However, successful redesign efforts rarely show this to be true. These skill sets are often more complex than initially thought, and oversight of the unlicensed individual must also be factored into the equation.

Another confounding variable can be the existence of collective bargaining units within an organization. Based on the amount of education required to produce competent unlicensed personnel, the supervision required from licensed staff, as well as the need to address the collective bargaining issue, Gundersen Lutheran made the decision to expand the use of licensed practical nurses rather than create a new role for unlicensed personnel.

The VAMC confronted the same types of issues in designing its new primary care model. Nurses who were comfortable in the acute care setting were not comfortable or competent in the clinic setting. Nurses who were able to provide care in medical-surgical units were not comfortable or competent to care for patients in the psychiatry area.

The increasing demand for in-depth knowledge related to specific patient populations makes it increasingly difficult to move nurses across clinical services or settings. Successful organizations recognize that nurses are not simply technicians, they are knowledge workers. As such, the old paradigm of "a nurse is a nurse is a nurse" is no longer operative. Successful organizations commit to intensive orientation programs and develop structured processes to document the competency set needed for each patient population and then ensure that only nurses with those skills are assigned to those patients. Some organizations may perceive this as limiting flexibility and, as such, decreasing efficiency. To the contrary, the data from these case studies indicate that this is a requirement for success—when the definition of success includes cost, quality, and access.

Biegen, Goode, and Reed, in their article "Nurse Staffing and Patient Outcomes," provide an excellent overview of a number of studies that address how changes in nursing care delivery systems can minimize adverse patient outcomes.[7] They conclude that staffing of patient care units must correspond to the unique needs of the patients on the unit and to existing data in the literature that indicate the level of staffing required to achieve the desired outcomes.

Training in Managing Work Groups   There is no simple answer to the issue of developing a high-quality, cost-effective health care delivery system. Providing appropriate educational training for licensed and unlicensed personnel and developing systems to document the clinical competence of licensed staff to care for specific patient populations will always be part of the process. Equally important, but most often overlooked, is providing training in areas of managing culturally diverse work groups; managing work groups with varying work ethics; and managing teams with strongly held and divergent values about patient care issues. The important thing is to recognize that to develop a well-prepared workforce capable of providing high-quality, patient-centered care requires a significant commitment of time to educate everyone involved in the process.

Developing an Empowered Workforce

Patient-centered care, process improvement work reorganization, cross-functional teams, customer-focused work teams, and employee-responsive management teams are common topics of discussion among health care providers and administrators during reengineering projects. An essential element to success in all of these endeavors is having an environment or culture conducive to change and an empowered workforce capable and willing to make independent decisions. But as the case studies demonstrate, a simple desire by administrators to get employees "on the band wagon" and develop an active partnership among administration, management, and all levels of staff is not enough. In most health care facilities today, the disenfranchisement of health care workers is a major problem. Substantive changes must occur in the basic fabric of the organization and within each of its employees if empowerment of staff, and therefore decentralized decision making, is to occur.

Commitment to Patient-Centered Care   Patient-centered care is an attempt to reorient the provider–patient relationship— a relationship that, in part, is historically rooted in how hospitals are organized. This commitment recognizes that to improve the health of patients we must not only deal with those things that caregivers do for patients, but also the things that patients and their families do for themselves. To achieve this goal, we must substantially change how we do business. We must move organizations from being bureaucratic and provider focused to being patient centered and patient valued. One way to frame this transition can be found in the concepts seen in Carlzon's book *Moments of Truth*.[8]

"Moments of truth" are described as brief encounters between patients and front-line staff that set the tone for the entire institution in the patient's mind. In health care, these moments of truth are often life-and-death situations at the bedside that cannot wait for review by supervisors. Health care providers are usually comfortable in this realm of clinical decision making. However, in other realms of decision making, they are significantly less likely to act from a patient-centered perspective.

Examples of this are seen in the incredible number of policies, procedures, guidelines, and rules unrelated to direct patient care that hospitals use to regulate every activity and interaction. From a moments-of-truth perspective, all levels of hospital employees, in all their encounters with patients and families, must have the freedom to act or lose forever an opportunity to satisfy the patient. Therefore, health care workers must become capable of decentralized, independent decision making. In other words, they must become empowered.

Staff Members as Partners in the Redesign Initiative
Each of the case studies identifies the importance of developing and recognizing staff as essential partners in the redesign enterprise. The case study from Elmhurst Hospital provides some examples of how the staff felt empowered to make decisions, such as offering dinner vouchers or movie tickets to patients as incentives for early discharges. The Veterans Affairs Medical Center points out the activities it used to recognize staff for involvement in process improvement activities. However, as with the need for teamwork and collaboration, this desired state is often articulated during the redesign efforts, but it is rarely achieved.

As staff become involved in operational improvements, several interesting factors are identified:

1. *Often the workforce cannot articulate the organization's mission and philosophy.* This is important because without a clear understanding of the institution's mission and vision, there is no foundation or context for consistent decision making.
2. *The organization's structure affects how employees act.* Employees are very aware of both the formal and informal pecking order. Traditional management structures with multiple layers between the key decision makers—the front-line staff—and administration promote informal structures that circumvent formal channels. Frequently, this is demonstrated by "management by memo"—a technique that delays and diffuses decision making to the point at which one has to wonder how, or if, anything really gets done. In contrast, a moments-of-truth management style flattens the pyramid. It eliminates tiers of responsibility so that response to patient needs is more direct and rapid. Communication occurs vertically and horizontally among all rather than a few.
3. *A conflict often exists between written policies and procedures and an articulated goal of decentralized decision making.* For example, an institution may require a department head's or vice president's approval to replace a broken door key. This is a

simple but important difference between what the organization actually requires and what it articulates as its commitment to decentralized decision making. This conflict is not lost on staff members.

4. *Organizational consistency is often lacking.* That is, management needs to evaluate if it "walks the talk." It is easy to express the desire to have employees comfortable with risk taking. Yet, there are often examples within the organization of employees who had taken a risk and been "cut off at the knees" when they made a mistake. It is clear why there is often a history of distrust to overcome.

From this comes the recognition that to facilitate organizational redesign toward the provision of patient-centered, patient-valued care, there is a need to focus on creating an employee-centered, employee-valued environment. Even with a flattened organizational structure, appropriate policies and procedures, and a well-understood mission and vision, it is critical to focus time and attention on changing the role of managers and administrators throughout the organization. Thus, to provide the safe, nurturing environment necessary for building an empowered workforce, all levels of management need to change from a traditional format where they are seen as administration, decision makers, or surrogate CEOs to a moments-of-truth format where they are seen as facilitators for the real decision makers—the front-line staff. Therefore, a significant redefinition of the role of management is necessary.

McGraw Empowerment Model   A useful model for creating an empowered workforce is the McGraw Empowerment Model.[9] This model is built on the basic concepts presented by Abraham Maslow.[10] (See figure 7-1.) Maslow's "Hierarchy of Needs" describes behavior as motivated by unmet needs. The lowest level is physiological needs, followed by safety, social, self-esteem, and, finally, self-actualization needs. Higher-order needs, such as self-esteem and self-actualization, will not motivate behavior until basic needs, such as physiological and safety needs, have been satisfied. When the basic needs are satisfied and no longer provide an impetus for behavior, the unmet higher-level needs do.

In the McGraw model, empowerment and its antecedents—work environment, organizational security, organizational culture, and organizational esteem—are seen as parallel to self-actualization and its antecedents in Maslow's hierarchy of needs:

- *Work environment:* The organizational equivalent of physiological needs is the need for a clean, safe, comfortable work environment. Thus, a manager attempting to empower employees must first attend to the physical aspects of the workplace. If the workplace is unsafe (for example, night shift workers are mugged in the parking lot), employees are unlikely to rise to empowerment until the environment is made safe. It may seem like a minor issue, but the attention administration gives to cleanliness in the workplace helps to convey to the employees that they are valuable and deserving.

Figure 7-1. Comparison of Maslow's Hierarchy of Needs with McGraw's Empowerment Model

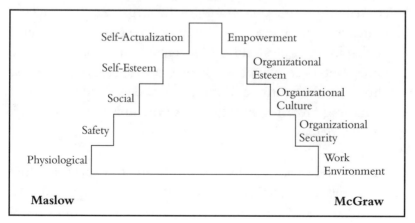

- *Organizational security:* A nonthreatening work environment, reasonable job security, and pervasive competence—having an expectation that all individuals in the organization will perform at an acceptable level and, if not, that disciplinary action will be taken—are parallel to safety in Maslow's hierarchy. If employees cannot trust the environment or each other to perform in a competent manner, it is doubtful that empowerment can survive. But how can an organization's leadership foster job security if there is none? Truth telling, impeccable attention to communicating information in a consistent and continuous manner, and acknowledging where uncertainty exists may be all a leader can do in an organization that is not sure of what the future holds.
- *Organizational culture:* This is the next level in McGraw's model and is comparable to Maslow's social needs. Organizational culture addresses the employees' sense of belonging, commitment, and acceptance within the organization. Leaders can foster a positive organizational culture by developing a formal system to involve employees in organizational and community activities.
- *Organizational esteem:* The level that immediately precedes empowerment in McGraw's model is organizational esteem. Organizational esteem, as with Maslow's self-esteem, reflects an individual's sense of recognition. Organizational esteem helps employees realize that their unique contributions are important to the organization's success. Managers can foster esteem by developing mechanisms such as thank-you notes and visible recognition for a job well done. But caution needs to be used to ensure that these efforts are substantive and not perceived as window dressing or playing favorites, in which case organizational esteem is actually decreased.

This model explains why it is unrealistic to expect employees to demonstrate empowered behavior until the prerequisite supports are in place. Empowerment, McGraw would say, is not a privilege or expectation established by administration. It is a natural progression in employee behaviors created by the clear actions of a committed administration.

Without security, employees are unlikely to undertake additional work or risk. Without trust, they are unlikely to suggest new ideas, try new processes, or act without direction from immediate supervisors. Empowerment, like self-actualization, can only occur when true organizational support of the individual has been proven over time. The culture of empowerment must become more than a promise. It becomes a reality when the organizational antecedents to empowerment have been demonstrated over time. Successful organizations recognize this and act accordingly.

Maintaining a Comprehensive Effort over Time

Successful redesign rarely results from a flash of inspiration. More often it is the culmination of a long-term journey. For example, the VAMC nurse executive's vision for the future was not a new idea: it matured over time. Then an opportunity presented itself in the guise of the mandate from headquarters for redesign. At that moment, as a respected leader, she was able to articulate her well-thought-out vision and move the institution forward.

It is important to recognize that resocializing an organization to a new culture with new roles and expectations, new skills to be learned, and new relationships to be created is not something that occurs overnight. Everyone wishes for an immediate turnaround, but successful redesign takes time. Although components of the projects were implemented quickly, the case studies in this book have been carried out over a number of years.

Beyond the commitment of time, there needs to be a commitment to providing the necessary resources for planning, training, and evaluating outcomes. For example, the VA facility recognized the need for a full-time coordinator to coordinate the overall efforts of all the individuals involved in the project. Failing to make a commitment to providing the time and other necessary resources to the project is one of the surest ways to ensure its failure.

However, commitment to sustain the redesign effort is easier said than done. Not only is time a factor, but so is the leaders' level of energy. Fatigue is often a problem as the leader continuously struggles to translate organizational changes into terms that relate to high-quality patient care services. It is critical that leaders recognize the drain on their energy supply and find ways to reinvigorate themselves as well as their staff. A leader cannot give to others what they do not have within themselves to give.

Many early redesign projects were focused solely on financial issues. The resultant simplistic approach of across-the-board budget cuts were rarely sustained over time. "FTE creep" and a returning to former ways of doing things were the inevitable outcome of this single-minded approach (to say nothing of the disillusionment of the participants). Therefore, even when financial viability is the motivating factor for change and expenses need to be reduced immediately, care must be taken to avoid focusing on early cost reduction without recognizing the importance of organizational mission and monitoring quality and service indicators. This simplistic cost-reduction approach is likely to drive out initial and essential commitment to providing the time and resources necessary to ensure that changes are both appropriate and sustainable over time.

Conclusion

According to Dr. W. Edwards Deming, author of *The Quality Revolution*, "There is no law that says anybody has to improve. It is all voluntary. It is only a matter of survival." Health care organizations are fighting for their very survival, so change they must. The question is how they choose to change.

Effective leaders will identify other organizations that have implemented successful redesign projects. The effective leader will look to these organizations for the lessons learned and the concepts developed that can be applied to the leader's own environment. The eight elements discussed in this chapter are common in successful redesign initiatives. Effective leaders recognize there is value in the work of others and will absorb the lessons and create their own successful future from which others will also learn. The journey has just begun.

References

1. K. Lewin, "Group Decision and Social Change," in *Readings in Social Psychology*, 3d ed., E. E. Maccoby, T. M. Newcomb, and E. L. Hartley, eds. (New York: Henry Holt, 1958), pp. 197–211.

2. F. L. Ulschak and S. M. SnowAntle, *Team Architecture: The Manager's Guide to Designing Effective Work Teams* (Ann Arbor, MI: Health Administration Press, 1995), p. 1.

3. J. B Harvey, *The Abilene Paradox and Other Meditations on Management* (San Francisco: Jossey-Bass, 1988).

4. J. R. Griffith, V. K. Sahney, and R. A. Mohr, *Reengineering Health Care: Building on CQI* (Ann Arbor, MI: Health Administration Press, 1995).

5. F. L. Ulschak and S. M. SnowAntle, *Team Architecture: The Manager's Guide to Designing Effective Work Teams* (Ann Arbor, MI: Health Administration Press, 1995).

6. S. Bucholz and T. Roth, *Creating the High Performance Team* (New York: John Wiley and Sons, 1987).

7. M. A. Biegen, C. J. Goode, and L. Reed, "Nurse Staffing and Patient Outcomes," *Nursing Research* 47, no. 1 (1998): 43–49.

8. J. Carlzon, *Moments of Truth* (Cambridge, MA: Ballinger Publishing Co., 1987).

9. J. McGraw, "The Road to Empowerment," *Nursing Administration Quarterly* 16 (1992): 16–19.

10. A. Maslow, *Motivation and Personality* (New York: Harper Bros., 1954).

CHAPTER EIGHT

Impact of Today's Redesign Initiatives on Tomorrow's Delivery of Health Care

Marjorie Beyers, PhD, RN, FAAN

One of the most important insights revealed by this book is that today's leaders are pioneers. The redesign initiatives described in the preceding chapters were designed and implemented by leaders. These leaders did not have role models; rather, they had a vision. The nature of change today is that new theories and practices are being developed and implemented through action experiments. This approach is quite different from former practices in which pilot programs were analyzed and refined before being carefully and slowly introduced. The once stable hospital structure has become an experiment in action in which every participant is a leader in introducing and refining change. One of the effects of this rapid introduction of change is that the playing field has been leveled. Everyone is involved in innovation. Instead of identifying and following the traditional definition of leader, everyone is leading some change. Current practice is characterized by new and varied models of nursing care delivery and variation in the expectations of leaders. Today's changes undoubtedly will influence the future. The challenge is to predict the direction of the impact.

This chapter discusses how the thinking behind health care delivery and the way it is currently organized is changing and how this will affect the role and competencies of nurses in the future.

Emerging Ways of Thinking about Health Care Delivery

Reflection on the future is facilitated by taking a step back to gain a broader view of health care delivery and to see more clearly the emerging way of thinking about the work of patient care and the role of health professionals. It is not fanciful to question the depth of the change. One could posit that the current change is preparation for an even more variable future in which practice and roles will continue to evolve in new ways. In this perspective, the current experiences have served to prepare for the future in several ways, including the following:

- The structures of health care organizations are being unbundled through work process improvements, formation of interdisciplinary cross-functional teams, consolidation of functions, and focus on outcomes.
- Focus on the patient has brought new meaning to the continuum of care and the goals of health for individuals and communities. The science of the continuum of care has more to do with processes and less to do with structure and settings.
- Practice has more to do now with making timely decisions supported by appropriate information, and less to do with following the rules or knowing what is the right way to accomplish the work according to predetermined policies and procedures.

- Structural elements of practice have given way to flexible team development to design and facilitate patient care. The previous concentration on right and wrong has given way to continuous improvement.
- Tools to help knowledge workers accomplish their work are now critical for effective functioning at every level of patient care. A new competency is learning how to use the knowledge in the new environment.
- The scope of practice has expanded to include more dimensions of patient care. Care providers now think in terms of clinical effectiveness, cost, and practicality in one package. Plans for innovations now include not only the goals but also the cost and value impact.
- Managerial roles now incorporate team building, coaching, and facilitating people to function rather than developing the plans for the work, making assignments, and monitoring progress.
- Career trajectories now center on expanding competencies rather than on achieving new titles or positions in an organization.
- Flexibility and mobility are highly valued characteristics in effective, responsive care delivery systems.
- Systems thinking is a core competency for health care professionals, giving new life to the concepts of care continuity and customization of services.
- Clinical competency is highly valued, reaching new levels of importance in health care organizations to achieve the expanding goals of health.
- Relationships for effective practice include interdisciplinary team players, patients, and community members in patient care planning and follow-through.

These insights indicate that future health care delivery systems will become increasingly dependent for effective practice on knowledge workers' functions. Organizations will be shaped to ensure that patients have access to care, participate in their own care, and provide input on what works and what needs to be improved. The bottom line for all of these insights is that care delivery will be shaped to meet patient needs for the total care experience. Elegant diagnosis and treatment will continue to be essential in the care processes, but the social aspects of health and illness care will be increasingly important to achieve high levels of patient satisfaction. Today's alternative care will be accepted practice as the scope of care interventions expands to wholeness.

Indications of the Changing Organization of Patient Care Delivery

The organization of the future is in embryonic stages. One example of a far-out notion of future organizations is provided by Pasternack and Viscio in their article "The Centerless Corporation: A Model for Tomorrow."[1] Imagine a global corporation that extends throughout the world, providing diverse services and producing diverse products held together by a core of services that support them. This corporation has no hierarchy and no complicated organizational charts. Rather, it is driven by the people who have the knowledge to perform. The financial controls and resource allocation are integral to the work of the service or product development. The locus of energy in this corporation is in the people who are performing. Information and insights are shared readily to facilitate improvement and innovation. Flexibility and responsiveness to new technology, changing demands, and new markets prevail. This type of organization is not too far-fetched when one examines some of the changes in attitude and valuing that have already begun within the hearts and souls of nurse leaders.

Some of the indications that nursing care delivery has already begun to move toward such an organization are presented below for consideration:

- *Time and space will be used very differently in the future.* Nurses working with patients across the continuum of care in ambulatory, home, and long-term care settings in addition to the hospital have already moved toward virtual practice. Being connected via computers, with access to patient information and resources for planning care and implementing care plans, helps these mobile nurses perform effectively wherever they may be. Thus, they are closer to patients and are moving their practice to the patients' environment rather than having patients come to a central structure for their care. Ask a Nurse programs were only the beginning of this movement. Community nursing centers and school and industrial health programs are yet another component. Using the Internet for health information, patient follow-up, and support has begun in many settings. The impact on patient care will be indicated by the way parameters of care are defined. Nurses, accustomed to being located in a hospital setting, have begun to develop practice patterns that are very different.

- *Knowledge will have different facets.* Learning how things are done will be supplanted by learning how to acquire knowledge, keep up to date, and apply knowledge to different contexts. The application of nursing knowledge will become less intertwined with organizational expectations for behaviors and more concerned with patient requirements for care. Professional practice models will profile the patient populations and corresponding care expertise required to shape a new form of specialization differentiated by principles and rationales rather than by how to perform procedures or use complex equipment. This prediction assumes a maturing technology that is easier to use and adapt to the needs of differing situations. Knowledge workers will incorporate continued learning in their practice, and their basic education will be the preparation for lifelong growth and learning.
- *The unbundling of boundaries, such as hours and locations of work, will require a new discipline for accomplishing work.* A benefit will be increased flexibility to match patient requirements for care and the personal styles and characteristics of caregivers.

The downside is that the work is not self-limiting. Health professionals will be engaged in complex processes and interactions with a new intensity. The introduction of e-mail and voice mail are examples of virtual communication without limits. As a consequence, there will be a greater need for safe havens—places or spaces where health professionals will take time to reflect on how to adapt knowledge in practice with increased focus and simplification. Working smarter to accomplish more with less is a good precursor to the way future demands must be managed.

- *Practice will become increasingly multivariate.* Approaching any management or care activity in a singular way will be ineffectual. The experience of today has proved the value of the "multis"—multidisciplinary, multicompetent, multidimensional, multisetting. In some cases, simplification will be achieved through consolidating the multis into one. In other cases, the combinations of expertise or function may be essential to achieve the outcomes. The main effect will be a new definition of specialization. The core patient care competencies will be increasingly well defined and refined through practice. The differentiating competencies for specialization will be continuously scrutinized against new technological developments and situations of care. Modular approaches will become increasingly popular, giving leaders the opportunity to form new combinations and new configurations that emerge with experience.

- *Simplification of structures and processes will continue to be a goal so as to create reasonable expectations for performance and to allow for their management.* New ways to define competencies, measure performance, and provide feedback and peer review will be developed with the support of information technology. Accountability for performance will be increasingly clear as data are used to profile practice patterns. A benefit is clarity in goal setting and improvement. A downside is that there will be little free space in performance. The interdependence of teams and work groups will emphasize the process and outcome evaluations as a way to discover new and improved means of providing patient care. A new type of socialization will emerge to support caregivers and patients in intense care situations.

- *Success will be measured based on performance and leverage rather than on posture or position within the organization.*[2] The basic educational processes and ongoing, lifelong learning essential to effective practice will look very different compared to present practice. The curriculum content will be increasingly varied, and options in the mode of study and the sequence of study will prevail. Faculty roles will emphasize research, relationships, and facilitation of learning in virtual learning environments. Faculty will be designated according to demonstrated expertise and practice capability. Learners will have options in selecting the source of information, mentoring, and support in their learning. The performance standards and measures will be refined to allow this flexibility in the learning process. The program of learning will begin with an assessment of characteristics, strengths, and propensities for behaviors that learners and mentors will use to guide the leaning process. Learning how to access data and information and then applying them will be part of the core curriculum. Developing the science will continue to require the work of dedicated researchers, with increasing involvement of practitioners in the care arenas.
- *Predictability will be highly valued but defined in different ways.* The focus will be on predicting parameters rather than specific events. Best practices will be incorporated into processes, to become automatic. Adaptation to varying patient care requirements will challenge the health professional. Organizing and depicting patient requirements for care will be facilitated by newly developing taxonomies of patient need. Although diseases and illnesses will continue to have names, symptoms, and syndromes, health professionals will focus on cause-and-effect relationships, risk, and potential for improvement. The social and psychological

aspects of wellness will be integrated into the caring approaches used. There will be patients with daily living support needs and those with needs for incremental assistance over time as aging and illnesses progress. These people will continue to require the intimate, traditional care to meet basic needs. New technology will be developed to assist health professionals with the emerging fields of community health interventions and empowering patients to participate in self-care. Future health professionals will be attuned to epidemiologic trends and interventions to anticipate and deal with health issues and problems.

Implications of Change on Nursing Roles and Competencies

Although difficult to believe, there is a cohort of nurses who have never known the past. Those entering the profession in this time of rapid and significant change have begun their careers in an environment of change. They have been introduced to a world of professional practice characterized by adaptation and innovation. Attention has shifted from the newly entering professionals to entry of seasoned and experienced professionals into the future. Many of the same insights developed around the transition from education to practice can now be applied to the transition from traditional to innovative ways of providing patient care.[3] There is a need to bridge gaps, initiate the new culture of health care, and formalize new parameters for evaluating professional practice and the outcomes. Leaders must now attend to their own transition to the future New career trajectories will be conceptualized and implemented in the future practice.

Implications for change have two main dimensions for professional growth: the dimension of education and the next iteration of empowerment:

• *Dimension of education.* Basic education will continue to incorporate liberal arts and sciences and the professional nursing courses that form the core of practice. The clinical experiences critical to a firm foundation for continued growth and development will be a subject of debate and experimentation as the opportunities for professional roles expand to include the full spectrum of patient care. Competencies in the care of the sick will continue to be foundational, but new areas of specialty will be developed in environmental and community health care. Advanced practice nursing will become the norm as these nurses forge new scopes of practice and new relationships with all types of caregivers. There will be growth in the knowledge base as the science of nursing practice incorporates new aspects of caregiving and interventions to promote health and deal with risk prevention and care of the chronically ill, the aging, and the dying. The essence of nursing will continue to be the mainspring of practice in the areas of caring and compassion.

- *Next iteration of empowerment.* In the future, empowerment will be the norm; it will be expected that behaviors of managers and clinical leaders of all types become less organizationally interdependent and more clinically focused on varying patient populations. The composition of the nursing workforce will continue to be pluralistic, and the current, unresolved issues of entry to practice will give way to acceptance that nursing is a comprehensive service that utilizes the technical and professional competencies of individuals prepared in different ways.[4] Credentialing will be an ongoing aspect of practice, related to performance profiles and demonstration of continued professional growth. Tools for assessing progression will be accessible online for use by nurses in their own plan for career development and professional growth. In addition to traditional competency-based credentialing, there will be assessment of skills and talents that will allow selection of job opportunities that match the individual's unique capacities. The dynamic nature of knowledge and learning will provide energy for continuous improvement.

Conclusion

It can be posited that the massive restructuring and redesign of patient care delivery have paved the way for a very different future. Mechanisms for continuous evaluation, action learning, and improvement in care processes will provide the insights for behavioral change. The lessons learned through restructuring that are shared in this book are examples of the way nurses will relate to the health care delivery system, to one another, and to patients in the future. Opportunities for development are rich in learning and in stretching nurses to achieve. The most important change for the future is freeing nurses from some of the confining traditions to realize their personal and professional potential. Nursing care is about helping people realize their potential. In the future, nurses will be better equipped to use their own personal potential to keep health care dynamic and effective in changing contexts and complex environments.

References

1. B. A. Pasternack and A. J. Viscio, "The Centerless Corporation: A Model for Tomorrow," *Strategy & Business* 12 (third quarter 1998), Booz Allen & Hamilton, pp. 10–21 (except 17–18).

2. J. Pfeffer, "The Real Keys to High Performance," *Leader to Leader* 8 (spring 1998): 23–29.

3. S. Wetlaufer, "HBR Case Study: After the Layoffs, What Next?" *Harvard Business Review* 76, no. 5 (September/October 1998): 24–26, 28, 30, 34, 36, 38–40.

4. W. Wilkins, "Overcoming the Fear of the Unknown," *The Futurist* 32, no. 7 (October 1998): 60.

Index

Acute care in care management model, 94–99

Albany Medical Center Hospital
  achieving financial turnaround at, 119–120
  case management at, 134
  clinical pathways at, 133
  clinical performance improvement at, 129–138, 156, 157, 161, 163–164, 165–166
  communication at, 141–142
  competency planning at, 143
  coping with change at, 125–128
  decision making at, 121–122
  education at, 142–143
  impetus for change at, 117–118
  leadership style at, 124–125, 128–129
  long-range plans for improvement at, 122–124
  nursing division restructuring at, 120–128
  operational performance improvement at, 119–129
  patient care delivery system improvement at, 134–138
  patient-centered care model at, 138–141
  quality improvement at, 117–152
  service-line improvement, 131–132
  service quality improvement teams at, 133–134
  simulations in the work plan at, 145–146
  transition at, 142

American Federation of Government Employees (AFGE), 21, 27

American Nurses Association (ANA), 21, 27

Ancillary roles, decentralizing, 55–59

Care management
  population-based approach to, 93–94, 99–100
  reengineering patient care delivery system through, 89–115

Care management model
  acute care in, 94–99
  community-based, 101–104
  framework of, 92–93
  limitations of outcome evaluation, 109–110
  obtaining physician participation and buy-in, 107
  predicted outcomes and staffing requirements in, 99–101
  strengths of, 91–92
  weakness of, 92

Case associates
  education and training for, 53
  role of, 52

Case management teams, 96–97

Case managers, 13, 134
  designing role of, 95
  education and training for, 53, 106
  recruiting qualified, 106
  role of, 52

Change, developing mechanisms for coping with, 125–128

Child life specialist, emergence of, 7

Clinical competency, training in, 167–169

Clinical outcome data, population profiles as method for presenting, 110–113
Clinical pathways, 133
Clinical performance improvement, developing capability for, 129–138
Clinical plans, 96, 98–99
Clinical practice standards, 98
Collaboration, demonstrating, 162–164
Community-based case management, 101–104
Community wellness program, 91
Competency planning, 143
Continuous quality improvement, 21, 90
Critical pathway development and implementation, 13

Data-driven process, 165–166
Decision making
developing new process for, 121–122
group process in, 82
Deming, W. Edwards, 176
Differentiated practice model, 50
decentralizing ancillary roles, 55–59
implementing pilot plan in, 59–63
professional nurse role in, 50–55
Disease management guidelines, 99

Education. *See also* Training
for case associates, 53
for case managers, 53, 106
patient, 26, 32–33
staff, 26, 32
Elmhurst Memorial Hospital
behavioral health services at, 78
cardiovascular services at, 77
continuum of care program at, 78–79
flattening of management structure at, 79–81
foundation for new organizational design at, 73
group decision making at, 82
health care teams at, 73–75
impetus for change at, 71–73
integrated team management model at, 71–88, 155–156, 158, 161, 162–163
leadership responsibilities at, 81–82
oncology services at, 78
outcomes at, 86–87
surgical services at, 77–78
team-think innovations and initiatives at, 82–84
trust in, 84–86
women's and children's services at, 78
Empowered workforce, developing, 169–175
Evaluation, identification of, as area for research and development, 26, 34–35

Fee-for-service model of health care, 4
as cost prohibitive, 6
factors contributing to, 4–5

Financial turnaround, achieving, 119–120
First-line managers, role of patient care executive in coaching, 12–13
Focus PDCA, 128

Gundersen Lutheran Hospital
decentralizing ancillary roles at, 55–59
decentralizing infusion therapy role at, 65–67
differentiated practice model at, 50–63
expansion of licensed practical nurse role at, 63–65
impetus for change at, 49–50
nursing culture at, 49–50
patient service assistant position at, 56–59
professional nurse role at, 50–55
responses to patient care needs at, 63–67
restructuring, to provide synergistic patient care, 49–68, 155, 158, 159, 163, 166, 168
staff retention rate at, 54–55

Health care costs at VA medical centers, 22–23
Health care delivery
attempts to reduce costs of, 6
emerging ways of thinking about, 180–182
impact of patient care redesign initiatives on, 179–188
making the transition from specialized, to primary care model, 19–45
need for accountability in, 6
Health care market, factors in precipitating a need for change in, 91
Health care premiums, increases in, 5–6
Health care teams, case for, 73–75
Hospital leadership, developing expectations for, 128–129
Hospital profile, 99

Informatics, identification of, as area for research and development, 26, 34
Infusion therapy role, decentralizing, 65–67
Inpatient case management, 97–98
Integrated team management model, 71–88
Interdisciplinary strategic growth plans, development of, 81–82

Joint Commission on Accreditation of Healthcare Organizations (JCAHO), 22

Kiersey Temperament Sorter, 85

Laborers International Union of North America (LIUNA), 21, 27
Lancaster General Hospital
acute care at, 94–99
case managers at, 106
community-based case management at, 101–104

impetus for change at, 90–91
obtaining physician participation and
buy-in, 107
population-based managed care approach
at, 93–94, 99–100
population profiles as method for presenting clinical outcome data, 110–113
predicted outcomes and staffing requirements, 99–101
reengineering patient care delivery system through care management at,
89–115, 156, 158, 166
Leadership
appointment of co-leaders, for primary
care teams, 31
developing expectations for hospital,
128–129
effecting changes in style of, 124–125,
128–129
guidance in developing skills of transformational, 44
responsibilities for, in integrated team
management model, 81–82
Licensed practical nurse, expansion of, 63–65
Long-range plans for improvement, mapping
out, 122–124

Managed care, nursing staff opposition to, 7
Management structure, flattening of, 79–81
Maslow, Abraham, 172
McGraw Empowerment Model, 172–175
Medical guidelines, 99
Mercer/HCIA list of "100 Top Hospitals:
Benchmarks for Success," 89
Multidisciplinary teams, 3

Nursing care, targeting for work redesign, 6
Nursing cost-centers, 6
Nursing executive, role of, in patient care
redesign, 3
Nursing framework, redesigning professional,
52
Nursing protocols, 99
Nursing roles and competencies, implications
of change on, 186–187
Nursing staff, opposition to managed care
and patient care redesign, 7

Occupational Safety and Health Administra-
tion (OSHA), 22
Operational performance improvement,
developing capability for, 119–129
Organizational culture, 174
before change to primary care, 20–22
Organizational vision, 50
Outcome evaluation, limitations of, 109–110

Patient care. *See also* Care management; Care
management model
responding to needs in, 63–67

restructuring to provide synergistic,
49–68
Patient care delivery
improvements in, 134–138
indications of the changing organization
of, 182–186
problems with traditional, 90
reengineering, through care management,
89–115
Patient care executive
attributes of, in successful work redesign,
7–13
in challenging assumptions, 8–9
in coaching first-line managers, 12–13
in creating adaptive environment, 9–11
in encouraging systems thinking, 11–12
in patient care redesign, 3–14
responsibilities of, 8–13
Patient care redesign. *See also* Work redesign
articulating clear purpose and vision for
the future, 158–160
data-driven or evidence-based process in,
165–166
demonstrating collaboration and teamwork in, 162–164
demonstrating willingness to invest in
training in, 166–169
developing empowered workforce in,
169–175
impact of, on health care delivery in,
179–188
implications of change in, on nursing
roles and competencies, 186–187
indications of changing organization on,
182–186
leadership with strong, positive personal
reputation in, 160–162
maintaining comprehensive effort over
time, 175–176
nursing staff opposition to, 7
patient care executive role in, 3–14
recognizing motivation for changing status quo, 156–158
staff members as partners in, 171–172
Patient care technician, 63–65
Patient-centered care model
patient care team system in, 139–141
patient expectations in, 138–139
Patient education, identification of, as area for
research and development, 26, 32–33
Patient expectations in patient-centered care
model, 138–139
Patient service assistant position
areas of responsibility for, 56–58
creation of, 56
evolution of, 62
job satisfaction among, 61
opposition to, 58–59
Physician participation and buy-in, obtaining,
for care management program, 107

Population-based managed care approach,
99–100
building foundation for, 93–94
Population profiles as method for presenting
clinical outcome data, 110–113
Press-Ganey patient satisfaction scores, 157
Primary care
development of implementation plan for,
26–27
making the transition from specialized
care delivery to, 19–45
organizational culture before the change
to, 20–22
Professional nurse, role of, 50–55
Professional nursing, redesigning framework
for, 52

Quality assurance, 21
Quality improvement, creating high performance through, 117–152

Reductions in force (RIFs), 20
Registered nurse, differentiation of role, 50
Respiratory therapist, emergence of, 7
RN project coordinator, appointment of, 26

Self-directed work teams, need for research
on, 44
Service-line improvement, 131–132
Service quality improvement teams, 133–134
Simulations, use of, in work plan, 145–146
Social workers, emergence of, 7
Space, identification of, as area for research
and development, 26, 34
Specialized care delivery, making the transi-
tion from, to primary care model,
19–45
Staff education, identification of, as area for
research and development, 26, 32
Synchronized interdependence, goal of, 74
Synergistic patient care, restructuring to pro-
vide, 49–68
Systems thinking, role of patient care execu-
tive in encouraging, 11–12

Teams
case management, 96–97
health care, 73–75
integrated management model for,
71–88, 155–156, 158, 161, 162–163
multidisciplinary, 3
patient care, in patient-centered care
model, 139–141
self-directed work, 44
service quality improvement, 133–134
Team-think innovations and initiatives, 72,
82–84

Teamwork, demonstrating, 162–164
Total quality management (TQM), 3, 6, 118
focus of, 118
Training. See also Education
for case associates, 53
for case managers, 53
in clinical competency, 167–169
demonstrating willingness to invest in,
166–169
in managing work groups, 169
Transformational leadership, guidance in
developing skills of, 44

VA medical centers, cost of care at, 22–23
Veterans Affairs Medical Center
co-leaders for primary care teams at, 31
evaluation phase in, 39–43
evaluation subgroup at, 34–35
health care model at, 28–30
impetus for change at, 22–25
implementation tasks, responsibilities and
decisions at, 30–31
informatics subgroup at, 34
key players in, 39
lessons learned at, 43–45
making the transition from specialized
care delivery to a primary care model
at, 19–45, 155, 157–158, 159, 160, 163,
168, 171–172, 175
organizational culture before change to
primary care at, 20–22
patient education subgroup at, 32–33
primary care implementation plan at,
26–27
primary care planning/implementation
group at, 25–26
progress and changes during
transition/implementation, 35–39
resource assessment at, 28
RN project coordinator at, 26
space subgroup at, 34
staff education subgroup at, 32

Workforce, developing empowered, 169–175
Work groups, training in managing, 169
Work plan, use of simulations in, 145–146
Work redesign. See also Patient care redesign
attributes of patient care executive role in
successful, 7–13
concept of, 3
essence of true, 13–14
introduction of, 5–7
targeting nursing care for, 6
Work restructure in providing synergistic
patient care, 49–68
Work simplification, 3